The Church of
the Firstborn
and the
Birthright

Kevin J. Conner

The Church of the Firstborn and the Birthright

Kevin J. Conner

CONNER
MINISTRIES

Published by Conner Ministries Ltd

CONNER
MINISTRIES

WEB: kevinconner.org
Email: kevin.conner321@gmail.com

Visit www.amazon.com/author/kevinjconner for a list of
other books by Kevin Conner.

Contents

Foreword

As I sat in the session and listened to the speaker something began to happen in my heart, something which was to change the course of my ministry to the church of the Lord Jesus. I have always valued the church and its supremacy in a given locality under the direction of Jesus, Who is the Head of the body of Christ. Yet as I listened to this excellent presentation a whole new and more meaningful appreciation of the church began to develop in my spirit. I began to see more clearly the important role the church plays in God's economy and in the world around us. I began to see that a beautiful, glorious church is the purpose of God in the earth, and that He is unfolding His plan through His church. It was like the beginning of a new day for me, a preacher of many years.

I turned to my wife, Evelyn, and said, "We have to have this ministry presented to our church, to share with others what we are hearing. These truths are vital to the growth and development of the house of God!" And thus it was that we had the joy of meeting our dear brother, Kevin Conner. Eventually he came to our church and gave his presentation of "The Church of the Firstborn," the recordings of which became the basis of this book. We have come to know Brother Conner as a man of God, and a man of the Word. His sincerity and love for the Lord have been a great blessing each time he has been with us. We count it a real joy and privilege to consider him our friend and fellow-minister of the Gospel. He will always be warmly welcomed into our church for fellowship in the Word.

As I have looked at the Church of the Firstborn and the Birthright with Brother Conner, the Bible, and especially the Old Testament, has come alive and taken on new meaning in a way it never had before. Many scattered Scriptures have fit together as God has given a more thorough revelation of the Word. This study is like "eye salve," lifting the scales from our eyes and causing us to see better the plan of God throughout both the Old and the New Testament. It has given all our efforts a more definite, motivating purpose. I trust that these truths will bless you as they have blessed us and our church.

We are living in great days when Jesus is restoring and building His church, and the future is bright under God. He is preparing a glorious church, and it's great to be part of it. Remember, the church of Jesus is not an afterthought -- it is an important part of God's plan and has been right from the beginning. Jesus will have a church that will rule and reign with Him throughout eternity. Be sure to get involved in it and give it everything you have, for it is the only worthwhile involvement in this life.

God bless you as you read this book! Through it, may the Lord increase your appreciation of His church and its significance in the earth in our day.

Daniel Straza
Regina, Saskatchewan, Canada
April 12, 1984

Chapter 1

God's
Firstborn Church

The Bible is God's Word; it is the Seed of God, or God's "Seed Book." As we study the Word of God we discover that in the book of Genesis, which is the "seed book" of the Bible, God has planted many tremendous seeds of truth. These seeds are watered and developed by the Spirit of God, growing throughout the entire Biblical revelation. Through Exodus, Leviticus, and so on they grow, through all the books of the Bible. Finally in the book of Revelation, "The Book of Ultimates," the growth is consummated.

One of the most exciting themes God has planted in His Word is that which pertains to *"The Church of the Firstborn."* In this present edition we will see the significance of this great subject and how it relates to the day we are living in. The portion of Scripture which will be the base for our study is Hebrews 12:14-29. Verses 16 and 18-24 will be of particular interest to us, but the entire passage is quoted below from the Authorized Version to give us the immediate context: *"Follow peace with all men, and holiness, without which no man shall see the Lord: Looking diligently lest any man fail of the grace of God; lest any root of bitterness springing up trouble you, and thereby many be defiled; Lest there be any fornicator, or profane person, as Esau, who for one morsel of meat sold his birthright. For ye know how that afterward, when he would have inherited the blessing, he was rejected: for he found no place of repentance, though he sought it carefully with tears.*

"For ye are not come unto the mount that

might be touched, and that burned with fire, nor unto blackness, and darkness, and tempest, And the sound of a trumpet, and the voice of words; which voice they that heard intreated that the word should not be spoken to them any more: [*For they could not endure that which was commanded, And if so much as a beast touch the mountain, it shall be stoned, or thrust through with a dart: And so terrible was the sight, that Moses said, I exceedingly fear and quake:*] *But ye are come unto mount Sion, and unto the city of the living God, the heavenly Jerusalem, and to an innumerable company of angels, To the general assembly and CHURCH OF THE FIRSTBORN, which are written in heaven, and to God the Judge of all, and to the spirits of just men made perfect, and to Jesus the mediator of the new covenant, and to the blood of sprinkling, that speaketh better things than that of Abel."*

For many years I read this passage of Scripture asking myself various questions: What was the "birthright" that Esau sold? Does a Christian have a birthright? Can he sell it like the Hebrew believers are being tempted to do? Also, what is the Church of the Firstborn? Is it any church, or is it some distinctive church?

Then one day the Spirit of the Lord began to quicken me on the connection between *"The*

Church of the Firstborn" and *"The Birthright."*
As much research was done on this subject, I
received a whole new understanding of the
church. I saw that when a person is added to
the church, there is a spiritual birthright which
belongs to them. I saw that many Christians
are like Esau, selling their spiritual birthright
for a mess of pottage. They are selling out for
temporal, carnal, and material satisfaction
that will rob them of their place in the Church
of the Firstborn, unless they come quickly to
repentance.

Thus, we set out to answer these questions:
What is the Church of the Firstborn? Who
belongs to it? Do Christians have a birthright
and if so, what is it?

In verses 22-24 of the passage under consideration we discover that the writer to the
Hebrews (though there is a difference of
opinion, this writer was possibly Paul) tells us
that there are *nine* specific things which the
New Covenant believer has come unto. We
have come:

1. *Unto Zion* — NOT the earthly, geographical
location in Palestine (v. 22).
2. *Unto the heavenly Jerusalem* — the city of
the living God. NOT unto the earthly
Jerusalem, which is spiritually Sodom and

Egypt, and which was about to be destroyed by Prince Titus in A.D. 70 (v.22; cf. Revelation 11:8; Matthew 24:1-2).

3. *Unto an innumerable company of angels* — angels who are ministering spirits sent unto the heirs of salvation (v.22; cf. Hebrews 1:14).

4. *Unto the general assembly* — the total redeemed company of saints, touching both Old and New Testament saints both in heaven and on earth (v.23).

5. *Unto the Church of the Firstborn* — the theme of our study (v.23).

6. *Unto God the Judge of all* — the true and living God, the Judge of all men (v.23).

7. *Unto the spirits of just men made perfect* — the saints who have departed from the earth and are now with the Lord (v.23).

8. *Unto Jesus the Mediator of the New Covenant* — NOT to Moses the mediator of the Old Covenant (v.24).

9. *Unto the blood of sprinkling* — the blood of Jesus Christ which speaks better things than that of Abel (v.24).

Each of these nine things we have come unto are vast subjects in themselves. However, it is the fifth one which is the theme we will pursue together, that is, The Church of the Firstborn.

The Church of the Firstborn

The Hebrew believers had been under the Old Covenant economy. Earthly Zion and Jerusalem had been their joy. Angelic visitations had been evidenced in the history of their nation. They knew what was involved in the general assembly of the tribes during the festival occasions. As a nation they had received the revelation of the true and living God. They knew about the blood of sprinkling. They knew that the saints who died in faith would, in due time, be taken into the presence of the Lord. Their minds were saturated with the concept of the firstborn. Israel, as a nation, was spoken of as "The Church in the Wilderness" (Acts 7:38).

But now the Messiah had come and had abolished, by His sinless, once-for-all and perfect sacrifice, all the ritualisms of the Mosaic economy. The writer to the Hebrews was endeavouring to wean them away from the earthly to the heavenly, from the carnal to the spiritual, from the shadows and types to the reality and antitype, from the animal sacrifices to the sacrifice of Jesus, from the Old Covenant to the New Covenant, and from the natural and national Israelite church to the spiritual Israelite church.

Many had been cast out of the synagogues. They had left the external for the internal, the natural for the spiritual. They were being tempted to lapse back into Judaism and forsake the New Covenant Christ of God. The writer warns them not to sell out their "birthright" in Christ for the "mess of pottage" that Judaism was offering. They had come to the glorious New Covenant realities -- they were called to be of the Church of the Firstborn ones, to inherit the spiritual and eternal birthright in Christ, the One to Whom Moses pointed. Why forsake it all to go back to the Old Covenant pottage? The same exhortation holds good for all believers today.

We ask ourselves therefore, "What is this Church of the Firstborn?"

In the New Testament we find there are various designations for "The Church." It is spoken of as "The Church," "The Church of God," and "The Church of God in Christ." It is often named after the locality in which the church is found, that is, "The Church of Ephesus," "The Church at Corinth," or "The Churches in Asia."

However, this peculiar title, *"The Church of the Firstborn,"* is only used once in the New Testament. As noted already, the Hebrew mind was saturated with the concept of the firstborn. As we go back to the roots of this concept, in the Old Testament, we find that there was one basic evidence of the importance of the firstborn: The firstborn always received special recognition and treatment. We will see that firstborn sons were shown preference in two particular ways. First, they were given the right to a special inheritance. This right is referred to as the "birthright." All sons could receive an inheritance, but the inheritance or birthright which was set aside for the firstborn was always far greater than that of the other sons. This special birthright automatically belonged to the firstborn, but it was possible for him to forfeit or sell this privilege.

The firstborn's birthright included a double portion of his father's material possessions (see Deuteronomy 21:17). This meant that if there were two sons, the firstborn received two thirds of the inheritance, while the other son received one third of it. Also, the birthright included the right of headship. If the father died or was absent, the firstborn was recognized as the head of the family (for example, Reuben in Genesis 37:21-30). Each son was head of his own family, but when the father died, the firstborn son inherited the headship of the father over all his brothers. Other privileges of the birthright will be discussed later in this study.

The second way the firstborn was given special treatment was that his father gave him a special, verbal blessing -- the "birthright blessing." Each son was entitled to a blessing, but the firstborn received this special blessing. The blessing of the father did more than simply pass on the inheritance; it also influenced the courses of the lives of his sons and their families, far into the future. The father could give a positive blessing or a negative curse but the birthright blessing was treasured because it was always positive and abundant, confirming the special benefits which were the portion of the firstborn.

When we study the early history of Israel, we discover that God gave some very important laws concerning the firstborn. A consideration of these will show the significance of the firstborn in God's mind and help us to understand the importance of *"The Church of the Firstborn."*

1. The firstborn were *sanctified* unto the Lord (see Exodus 13:1-2). Whether born of man or beast, the Lord claimed the firstborn as His. They were sanctified, set apart, separated unto God from the moment of their birth. None could have the firstborn, for they were separated exclusively unto the Lord.

2. The firstborn of animals were presented to the Lord by *sacrifice* (see Exodus 13:11-13). As far as the firstborn of donkey animals were concerned, they were to be redeemed by the sacrifice of a lamb. This pointed to the fact that the firstborn needed redemption by blood sacrifice. If the donkey was not redeemed by the lamb, then its neck was broken. All this points to the fact that mankind, like the stubborn, willful, and rebellious donkey, needs redemption by the blood of the Lamb of God (see John 1:29,36).

3. The firstborn sons were *presented* to the Lord (see Exodus 13:12,13; 22:29). God claimed all firstborn sons as His own property.

4. The firstborn were *redeemed* (see Exodus 13:13). To be redeemed means to be bought back for a price, the price of redemption.

5. The firstborn were *hallowed* unto the Lord (see Numbers 3:11-13). Hallowed means to be made holy unto the Lord, and is linked with the thought of sanctification.

The study of these Scriptures therefore shows us the importance of the firstborn in the mind of God. The nation of Israel, by the laws of God, became aware of the significance of all the firstborn, whether of man or beasts. The firstborn were sanctified, sacrificed, presented, redeemed and hallowed to God.

These laws help us to appreciate the truth of what is implied by *"The Church of the First-born"* spoken of in Hebrews. This church will be:

* *A CHURCH* that is *SANCTIFIED* unto the Lord (see Ephesians 5:26; I Thessalonians 5:23);

* *A CHURCH* that is *SACRIFICED* unto the Lord as a living sacrifice (see Romans 12:1);

* *A CHURCH* that is *PRESENTED* to the Lord without spot, or wrinkle, or blemish, or any such thing (see Ephesians 5:25-27);

* *A CHURCH* that is *REDEEMED* by the blood of the Lamb of God (see Titus 2:14 and Hebrews 9:14);

* *A CHURCH* that is *HALLOWED* or made holy before the Lord (see Hebrews 12:10,14; and Ephesians 5:27).

This is the kind of church Christ is building. He said *"upon this rock I will build MY CHURCH: and the gates of hell shall not prevail against it"* (Matthew 16:18b).

The church, as God's "CALLED-OUT COMPANY," will be a church which measures up to the Divine standard. It is possible to belong to a denomination and not belong to His church, and it is possible to belong to His church, yet not to a denomination.

When a person is genuinely born again, born

from above, born into the kingdom of God
(John 3:3-5), and "added to the church" (Acts
2:47), he becomes a member of the "Church of
the Firstborn," and obtains from the Lord his
spiritual "Birthright."

Chapter 2

The Last
Shall Be First

There is another Divine principle which clearly relates to the Church of the Firstborn.

In Matthew's Gospel we have the account of Peter, along with the other apostles, telling Jesus how much they had forsaken to follow

Him. The Lord Jesus reminded them that they would be well recompensed, not only in this life, but in the life to come, for any sacrifices they had made for His sake and the Gospel. As He said this, He made a very peculiar statement, saying, *"But many that are FIRST shall be LAST; and the LAST shall be FIRST"* (Matthew 19:30).

The truth of this parable is evident in our day. Many are coming unto the Lord in these "last days," in "harvest time," and are receiving from the Lord the same truths and blessings which others, who have laboured for years in the Gospel, are now receiving or have received. The Lord is the Lord of the harvest. It is the harvest He is concerned about.

However, the principle which we are considering in relation to the Church of the First-born is that which has been quoted from Matthew 19:30 and 20:16: *"The LAST shall be FIRST, and the FIRST LAST."*

This divine principle is applicable to our theme, as we will see in a number of accounts in the Old Testament where this Divine principle applies. It will be seen that, in God's mind, that which is *first* in man's eyes, becomes *last* in His eyes. That which is first (after the flesh) manifests certain characteristics, so God sets it to be last, while that which is last (in man's eyes), God sets to be first.

Cain and Abel

Genesis chapter four gives us the account of the first two sons of Adam and Eve, whose names were Cain and Abel. Cain was the older brother, the firstborn after the flesh, while Abel was born second. However, that which is firstborn after the flesh is not necessarily the firstborn after the Spirit, as far as God is concerned. In this situation we will see that the "first will be last, and the last will be first."

Now, in the process of time, Cain and Abel brought their sacrificial offerings to the Lord at the Gate of Eden before the flaming sword of the Cherubim, which may have been the Tabernacle or Sanctuary of the Lord until the time of the Flood. The end result was that the Lord accepted the offering of Abel and rejected that of Cain. It is possible that fire came out from the Shekinah Glory Presence of the Lord sealing the sacrifice of Abel in acceptance. Though God pled with Cain, and told

him that he could still have the rights of rulership (the rights of the firstborn), Cain rebelled
and in anger murdered his brother (see Genesis
4:7,8). Then, when God called to him, Cain
tried to plead innocence with regard to the
whole matter. God then placed a mark on
Cain and drove him from His presence.

We may ask, "Why did God reject Cain's
offering and accept Abel's?" The following
important points should be noted in answer to
this valid question.

The Offering of Cain
* Cain must have heard the Gospel from
Adam. This means he would have understood
the reason for the Fall, and God's gift of atonement by blood sacrifice. God symbolically
displayed justification by faith in the atonement when He clothed Adam and Eve with the
coats of skin.
* Cain had not allowed the "word of the
Gospel" to create faith in his heart.
* Cain brought the fruit of the ground, that is,
fruit from the ground that had been cursed by
God.
* Cain brought an offering that he had pro-
duced by the sweat of his brow. It was the
product of his own works.
* Cain was a religious man and came to worship God by way of self-effort.

* Cain's offering was a bloodless offering, but there is no way to approach God apart from blood atonement.

* Cain was a liar and a murderer, taking on himself the characteristics of the devil, who is a liar, murderer, and blood-of-the-lamb rejector.

The Offering of Abel

* Abel also must have heard the "word of the Gospel" from Adam and Eve. This would be the story of the Fall, of God's atoning grace and the way of approach He provided through the blood of a sacrificial victim.

* Abel allowed this word to create faith, for *"faith cometh by hearing, and hearing by the word of God"* (Romans 10:17). Abel made his offering by faith (Hebrews 11:4).

* Abel brought sacrificial victims. Thus a relationship was established between God and Abel through the body and blood of a sacrifice to God. Abel displayed faith in a blood atonement.

* Abel brought that which God had created - a lamb. It was nothing he had worked for, but something he had faith in, pointing to Christ THE LAMB of God (see John 1:36).

* Abel was a faith-righteous man (see Matthew 23:35, I John 3:12, and Hebrews 11:4).

* Abel was willing to die for his faith in God,

and became the first martyr.

* Abel was accepted of God because of his righteousness, while Cain was rejected because his works were evil (see I John 3:10-12).

Thus we have the "way of Cain" and the "way of Abel" (see I John 3:12 and Jude 11). All mankind follows one way or the other. One is the way of works, and the other is the way of faith. One is trusting in what self can do, the other is trusting in what God can do. Abel was trusting God through the death of another. Cain trusted himself in what he could do to make himself presentable to God. Somewhere in Cain's heart the devil had planted an evil seed. Thus, Cain was rejected of God.

We notice here the characteristics of the *FIRSTBORN AFTER THE FLESH*. These are manifested in Cain, the firstborn after the flesh, who is *REJECTED* of God, or set aside. Abel, who was second born, is *ACCEPTED* of God, and in God's eyes, would have become the firstborn. However, since Abel was murdered by Cain, God replaced him with Seth, who is brought in as a substitute seed (see Genesis 4:25).

Thus we see the Divine principle in Adam's first two sons, the FIRST shall be LAST, and the LAST becomes the FIRST. The rights of the firstborn, which include rulership and the birthright inheritance, are taken from Cain. These are given to another by the Lord.

Abel exemplifies the characteristics of the *FIRSTBORN AFTER THE SPIRIT!* He is a man of faith, a man who believes in blood atonement, and a man accepted of God as faith-righteous. The Church of the Firstborn will be characterized by such qualities before God. The church that follows the way of Cain — The False Church — will be rejected of God. And although it may be FIRST in man's eyes, it will be the LAST in the eyes of God, for it is a blood-of-the-Lamb rejector and murderous indeed (see Revelation 17). The True Church which is LAST in man's eyes, will be THE CHURCH OF THE FIRSTBORN in the truest sense of that expression. "The FIRST shall be LAST and the LAST shall be FIRST." Cain was first but became the last. Abel was last but became the first! Seth, the substitute seed, carried on the rights of the firstborn in the line of faith (see Genesis 4:25).

Ham and Shem

Just as Adam had three sons, Cain, Abel,

and then Seth, so we see a similar pattern in Noah, the next father of the human race. Noah had three sons, Shem, Ham, and Japheth (see Genesis 9,10,11).

Again we see the Divine principle manifested here. The characteristics of the *firstborn after the flesh* are seen in Ham (even though he was the younger son) and Shem manifests the characteristics of the *firstborn after the Spirit*.

In Genesis 9:18-27 we have the short account of the terrible sin of Ham with relation to his father, Noah. It should be remembered that although Ham is spoken of as the younger son, it is in him that the characteristics of the evil one are seen. These are the characteristics of the firstborn after the flesh, those of the natural and unregenerate man, which pertain to the first birth!

After the Flood, Noah planted a vineyard, took of the fruit of the vine, and got drunk. Whether Noah knew anything about the fruit of the vine causing drunkenness we do not know. Nevertheless, in his drunkenness Noah became naked. Drunkenness and immorality are often linked in Scripture.

It is also worthwhile to note that both fathers, Adam and Noah, sinned by a tree and its fruit. Both Adam and Noah brought a curse on their offspring. Both Adam and Noah were discovered in their nakedness after partaking of the fruit of a tree. Both Adam and Noah were covenant men, and received promises of redemption from God in spite of their sinfulness. Both Adam and Noah were fathers of the human race, destined to replenish and fill the whole earth. We note now some of the main characteristics of Ham and of Shem and their link-up with the principles of the firstborn.

Characteristics of Ham

* Ham opened his mind to the thoughts of an unclean spirit when he saw his father's nakedness.

* Ham talked about his father's nakedness to his two brothers, Shem and Japheth.

* Ham dishonoured his father by all he said and did.

* Ham comes under the curse of God through Noah, and this curse is passed on to his offspring. He is rejected of God. As Cain came under the curse of God, so does Ham (see Genesis 9:20-25).

Characteristics of Shem

* Shem, along with Japheth, did not respond to Ham's evil report of their father. They did not become curious about their father's nakedness or yield to the unclean spirit and talk about it.

* Shem, with Japheth, walked backwards and covered their father's nakedness, thus honour-

ing and respecting their father. The first com-
mandment with a promise is to honour father
and mother. It has a promise of long life with
it (see Exodus 20:12; cf. Ephesians 6:1-4).

* Shem, along with Japheth, is blessed of the
Lord God and Shem becomes the progenitor of
the Messiah (see Genesis 9:26,27). Shem
receives the promise that is due to the firstborn to be part of the seed-line for the Messiah
to come through. Thus, though God records
the sin of Noah, He allows a prophetic word to
come over each of his sons, involving blessing
and cursing accordingly. Both Ham and
Adam's son Cain come under the curse of God,
and thus are linked by this characteristic. The
pattern is here. Even though Ham is not the
firstborn naturally, he does take on the characteristics manifested in Cain. Shem becomes
the firstborn in God's eyes and is given the
birthright involving the Messianic seed. By
Divine principle, "the first becomes the last,
and the last becomes the first." The pattern
thus continues through the generations, and we
come to Abraham and his sons, Ishmael and
Isaac.

Ishmael and Isaac

The Divine pattern is very clearly seen in Genesis 16-21 regarding these two sons of Abraham, who is the father of all who believe. Ishmael is the firstborn after the flesh, with relation to the natural birth. Isaac is the last with relation to the natural birth, yet he replaces Ishmael, and thus becomes God's firstborn. Let us note some of the characteristics which God has recorded in His holy Word which show why Isaac becomes the firstborn after the Spirit, while Ishmael is set aside.

Characteristics of Ishmael

* Ishmael was born as a result of a union with Hagar, the Egyptian. Hagar was not a proper wife, but was an Egyptian bondmaid.

* Ishmael was the evidence of man's self-effort, endeavouring to make God's Word work. It was man trying to fulfil the promises of God by his own efforts.

* Ishmael mocked Isaac, the son of promise, when Isaac was born and weaned.

* Ishmael, in due time, had to be cast out, for he was the son of the bondwoman, and therefore a bondson. He could not be the true heir of the promises of God.

* Ishmael was characterized by the way he despised that which was born of promise by the power of the Spirit.

* Paul uses Ishmael and Isaac in an inspired allegory as being significant of the two covenants. Ishmael characterizes the Old Covenant of the Law, and Isaac characterizes the New Covenant of Grace (see Galatians 4:21-31). Abraham, through impatience, went in to Hagar and thus Ishmael was born. He was not the fulfilment of God's promise, for the promise was that Sarah would have a son. This son was to be born in God's time. We inherit the promises of God by faith and patience (Hebrews 6:12). As a result of Abraham's impatience Ishmael was born, and was nothing but trouble. In due time, when Isaac was born and weaned, God told Abraham and Sarah to cast out Ishmael, as he could not be the heir of the Divine promises. Though Ishmael was firstborn after the flesh, he was set aside by God so that God could bring in His firstborn, Isaac.

Characteristics of Isaac

* Isaac is the son of promise, born as a result of a miracle of God in the lives of Abraham and Sarah.

* Isaac manifests the characteristics of an obedient son of promise. In this he is used as a

type of the Only Begotten Son of God (see John 3:16).

* Isaac was a beloved son who was eventually offered, in type, as a sacrifice to God on Mount Moriah. Figuratively, he was raised from the dead. God had Abraham do typically, with his only begotten son, what He Himself, as the heavenly Father, would actually do with His Only Begotten Son, Jesus (see Hebrews 11:17-19).

* Isaac is a man of peace, a man of faith. These are characteristics of the Godly line.

* Isaac fulfils the promises of the covenant of God, and eventually Jesus, the New Testament Only Begotten Son, is born through his line.

There are many comparisons between Isaac and Jesus. Isaac shows forth characteristics which are typical of the Son of God, Jesus Christ. Isaac's name means "laughter," and what joy and laughter there was when Isaac was born. He becomes the true heir of the covenant promises. Paul, in his inspired allegory, likens him to the New Covenant sons, those born of the Spirit, those born of promise. He said that, as Ishmael mocked him who was born after the Spirit, so the Judaizing people mocked those who were born from above, born again. The Jews mocked the Christians. Those of the natural, fleshly birth of Abraham's seed mocked those who were born again after the spiritual, heavenly seed of Abraham.

The Lord promised Abraham that he would have seed as *the sand or dust* (Genesis 13:16), and then later that his seed would be *as the stars* (Genesis 15:5). After the typical death and resurrection of Isaac, God reverses the promises and puts *the star* seed *first*, and *the sand* seed *last* (see Genesis 22:17).

The sand seed represents the earthly, natural, national seed of Abraham, that seed which is after the flesh. It was multitudinous indeed.

The star seed represents the heavenly, spiritual, true Israel of God, which is the true seed of Abraham after the Spirit. This also is multitudinous indeed. Jesus told the Jews that, though they were Abraham's seed "after the flesh," they were not Abraham's seed "after the Spirit" because they would not believe Him (see John 8:37ff.).

Thus the pattern is consistent. Ishmael, firstborn after the flesh, is set aside. Isaac, lastborn after the flesh, becomes the firstborn after the Spirit. Here are two firstborn sons: Ishmael, firstborn of Hagar, and Isaac, first-born of Sarah — yet Isaac becomes the FIRST and Ishmael becomes the LAST! The sand seed which was FIRST becomes the LAST, and the

star seed which was LAST now becomes the
FIRST! These two sons represent two covenants. One is the covenant of works, of law,
and of legalism. The other is the covenant of
grace, and of faith.

Ishmael married into the line of Ham, who
had also been set aside. Therefore we find
that "flesh begets flesh." Isaac married into
the line of Shem, who was also firstborn after
the Spirit, and thus *that which is born of the
Spirit is spirit* (John 3:6b). Flesh can only
produce flesh. Spirit can only produce spirit.

The characteristics of Cain, Ham, and
Ishmael combined, together show why God
sets aside the firstborn after the flesh. The
characteristics of Abel, Seth, Shem, and Isaac
combined, together show why God chooses
them as members of His "Church of the Firstborn."

We go to the next example of this Divine
principle and pattern.

*Esau and
Jacob*

The pattern continues in Genesis 25-28.

After Isaac's marriage we find that his wife Rebekah conceived in due time. There was a struggle within her, and so she went to enquire of the Lord as to the reason. The Lord showed her that there were twins in her womb. These twins were two sons, two nations, two manner of people. One would be stronger than the other, and the elder would serve the younger.

In due time these twin sons were born, and they were named Esau and Jacob. We note some of the characteristics of these two sons and see why God sets aside the firstborn after the flesh and brings in His firstborn after the Spirit. Esau is set aside and Jacob is brought in. Thus the Lord says, "I am the God of *Abraham, the God of Isaac* (not Ishmael), and and the *God of Jacob* (not Esau)!"

Characteristics of Esau

* Esau was firstborn after the flesh. He was born a hairy man, and red all over.

* Esau grew up to be a wild man, a man of the field, a hunter.

* Esau was a man given over to carnal appetites of the flesh. He loved food. He was also a fornicator.

* Esau sold his birthright to Jacob for a mess of pottage. He despised his birthright and went his own way.

* Esau did not value spiritual or eternal things,

and repented too late when he found that his
father, Isaac, had blessed Jacob.

* Esau would have killed his brother, Jacob,
out of hatred, but Jacob was spared since it was
Esau, not Jacob, who despised the birthright
(see Hebrews 12:15-17).

* The writer to the Hebrews warns the Hebrew
believers not to be like Esau, who was the firstborn after the flesh but sold his birthright.

Thus we may say today, in allegorical lang-
uage, that there is a struggle going on in each
individual believer and in the church. The
struggle is between the flesh and the Spirit,
between Esau and Jacob. There are Christians
who, like Esau, are selling out their spiritual
birthright for a mess of pottage, for temporal
and carnal satisfactions. These Christians will
one day repent of it, but it will be too late to
change the Father's mind. *"Looking diligently
lest any man fail of the grace of God; lest any
root of bitterness springing up trouble you, and
thereby many be defiled; Lest there be any
fornicator, or profane person, as Esau, who for
one morsel of meat sold his birthright. For ye
know how that afterward, when he would
have inherited the blessing, he was rejected:
for he found no place of repentance, though he
sought it carefully with tears"* (Hebrews
12:15-17).

Characteristics of Jacob
* Jacob was born last after the flesh. He laid hold of Esau's heel at birth.
* Jacob was a plain, upright and sincere man. He was a family man.
* Jacob was a man of faith. He believed God and valued spiritual things.
* Jacob saw value in the birthright which Esau despised. He did not "steal" the birthright from Esau. Esau despised it and sold it to him for a meal.
* Although Jacob, at his mother's command, did deceive his father as to the birthright blessing, he did value spiritual and eternal things.
* He was punished for "doing a right thing a wrong way"; nevertheless God overruled in the whole matter and made Jacob the firstborn.
* Jacob was the one who received the new name, Israel, and became the Prince having power with God and men.
* Jacob is the one whom God delights to identify with, calling Himself, "The God of Jacob."

Thus the pattern continues. Jacob, firstborn in God's sight, receives the birthright. Esau, firstborn in man's sight, sells out his birthright and becomes a wild man. So today, there are those "Esau believers" who sell out their spiritual birthright for carnal pleasure. If they do not repent, they don't receive their birthright. There are also those "Jacob believers" who, in spite of their nature, deep down want God, and value the spiritual, eternal promises of the birthright. Just as Jacob and Esau were separated in due time, so there is coming a separation today in the church between the "Esau" and "Jacob" believers. God will have His Church of the Firstborn who will both value and inherit the birthright, by right of spiritual and heavenly birth.

Jacob laid hold of Esau's heel. This links him with the promise of Genesis 3:15, where the seed of the serpent would bruise the heel, and the seed of the woman would bruise the serpent's head. The head and the heel are connected at the birth of Esau and Jacob. Warfare was to be manifested between "the seed of the serpent" and "the seed of the woman." This is certainly evident in the pattern we have been following. Cain wars against Abel. Ham wars against Shem. Ishmael wars against Isaac, and Esau wars against Jacob. The firstborn of the flesh is enmity against the firstborn of the Spirit, the firstborn of God. Thus it is, has ever been, and shall be. In the last days, the Church of Man will war against the Church of God -- the TRUE CHURCH OF THE FIRSTBORN!

There will be two seed lines: The seed of the serpent and the seed of the woman. There will be two churches: The false and the true. There will be two firstborns: The firstborn after the flesh, and the firstborn after the Spirit.

Chapter 3

The Firstborn
of Nations

In Exodus chapters 3 and 4 we have the account of God's call of Moses to be His deliverer of His chosen people, Israel. A very important part of the Divine message given by the Lord to Moses concerned the theme of "The Firstborn." We note especially what these verses say: *"And thou shalt say unto Pharaoh, Thus saith the Lord, ISRAEL IS MY SON, EVEN MY FIRSTBORN: And I say unto thee, Let my son go, that he may serve me: and if thou refuse to let him go, behold, I WILL SLAY THY SON, EVEN THY FIRST-BORN"* (Exodus 4:22-23).

Now let us consider the tremendous implications of this passage. We are considering this glorious subject of "The Firstborn" on a national scale. We have two nations represented: Egypt and Israel. In Genesis God took two individuals. In Exodus He is taking two nations. In Genesis He set aside the firstborn in the natural and takes up the firstborn in the spiritual. In Exodus He sets aside the FIRST of the nations, Egypt, and takes up the LAST of the nations, Israel. Israel becomes God's firstborn, while Egypt becomes first and greatest of the worldly nations of antiquity. Israel was the smallest of the nations, even "few in number" (Deuteronomy 7:7), while Egypt was "firstborn" of the nations, but God says that "Israel is MY FIRSTBORN."

Israel is spoken of as *"THE CHURCH in the wilderness"* (Acts 7:38). In this passage in Exodus, Israel is spoken of as *"THE FIRST-BORN."* Thus we have the connection of these two thoughts and can say that Israel was the

Old Testament *"CHURCH OF THE FIRST-BORN"* in God's mind! God calls Israel My Son, My Firstborn, My Church. Israel becomes the "CALLED-OUT COMPANY," the "ekklesia," called out of Egypt into the wilderness to be joined to the Lord God in the marriage covenant: *"I will make a new covenant with the house of Israel, and with the house of Judah: Not according to the covenant that I made with their fathers in the day that I took them by the hand to bring them out of the land of Egypt; which my covenant they brake, although I was an husband unto them, saith the Lord"* (Jeremiah 31:31b-32). The Lord told Pharaoh that if he did not let His son, Israel, go, then He would slay Pharaoh's son, Egypt. Egypt was the greatest nation, the greatest national power, the greatest empire at this time, THE FIRST indeed! We will remember that Egypt came from the line of HAM! Thus we find that Egypt, as a nation, does what Cain did, and follows the way of Ham also. The evil characteristics of the firstborn after the flesh are manifest in Egypt.

Even to this day, we see how the Arab nations (of Ishmael, Ham, Esau, etc.) have great enmity with the Jewish nation (of Abraham, Isaac, Jacob, etc.). God has described the roots of this conflict in His Word, in

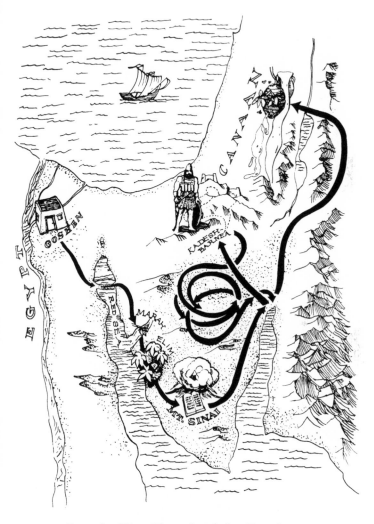

Israel: The Church of the Firstborn
in the Wilderness

the Divine and glorious pattern of the Firstborn! The only hope for both Arabs and Jews
is to find reconciliation in Christ, be born again
by the spiritual NEW BIRTH, and come into
that which is God's Church of the Firstborn
ones!

Now, in the passage in Exodus chapter 4,
there is something of great significance. The
Lord God said, Israel is MY SON, MY
FIRSTBORN!" Note--God did not say "The
Israelites are My sons" (plural), but "Israel is
MY SON" (singular). God takes a whole
nation, a collective people, a company of
people, a nation consisting of twelve tribes,
and says Israel is MY SON, MY FIRSTBORN!
Israel, as a NATION, is God's Son, His firstborn. *It is a many-membered Son! It is a
many-membered seed! It is a many-membered
Church of the Firstborn!*

Who can fail to see the glory of God's pattern
here on the national level? God said He would
smite Egypt; He would smite "thy son, even
thy firstborn." So Egypt, as a nation, a collective people, is spoken of in the singular also.
Egypt is a "many-membered son" and a "many-
membered firstborn." Thus Israel, as a nation,
is God's son, God's firstborn. Egypt, as a
nation, is also a son, a firstborn, that will be
smitten by God in judgment. It will be an

exchange of firstborn for firstborn.

This principle of singularity and plurality is used by the apostle Paul in his letter to the Galatian church. In Galatians 3:16,29 we have two thoughts brought together that attest to this truth. In verse 16 Paul says that the promises were to *"Abraham and his seed...not, And to seeds, as of many; but as of one, And to thy seed,* (singular) *which is Christ."* Christ is THE SEED of Abraham. Christ was THE FIRSTBORN of Mary, the first begotten of the Father, God. So the word "seed" is used in the singular in verse 16. However, when we drop to verse 29 we have the same word "seed" used in the *singular,* but applied to a company, a *plurality,* of people! *"And if ye* (plural) *be Christ's, then are ye* (plural) *Abraham's seed* (singular), *and heirs according to the promise."*

The believers in Christ, which are many, are brought together as part of that ONE SEED. Christ is THE SEED of Abraham. Believers in Christ are also THE SEED of Abraham. Thus, together, CHRIST AND THE CHURCH ARE THE SEED *of Abraham through whom the nations of the earth are to be blessed!* Christ is the Head, and the church is His body. United together as one, Christ and His body is that many-membered seed, that firstborn of God in the earth, who together will inherit the

glorious birthright of the firstborn. Christ and
His church constitute "the seed." The church
is a many-membered seed (see also I Corinthians 12:12). It is a many-membered firstborn. Hence, when God promised Abraham
that all nations and all families of the earth
would be blessed through his seed, He was
speaking of Christ and the church!

Israel was God's son, God's firstborn. Egypt,
as firstborn after the flesh and first of the
nations of earth, would be set aside, rejected of
God. Israel becomes a type of the New Testament church, the spiritual Israel of God.
Egypt becomes a type of the unregenerate of
mankind, and those who are set aside by God.

The Firstborn
Lamb

We come now to the real reason, the Divine
reason, why Egypt is set aside and Israel is
chosen to be God's Church of the Firstborn.
Exodus 11, 12, and 13 should be read carefully
with relation to the things considered here.
This message of the firstborn is given by the
Lord to Moses and to all of Egypt as well.

They have an opportunity to either accept or reject it.

We have seen that this message of the firstborn operates on the national level. Now we shall see it operate in the marvelous deliverance of Israel out of Egypt, the deliverance of God's "ekklesia" out of the house of bondage. The whole message and deliverance are again stamped with the concept of "The Firstborn." God will get the message through somehow.

In these chapters we see the Lord telling Moses to tell the Israelites that He was about to deliver them. They were to take a FIRST-BORN lamb, a lamb of the FIRST year, and FIRSTLING of the flock and keep it for four days, then kill it in the evening of the fourteenth day of the month. They were to take the blood of this Passover lamb and sprinkle it on the two side posts and lintel of the door of their houses. Then they were to feed upon the body of the lamb. At the midnight hour God would send an angel through to smite all the houses where no blood was to be seen. God would smite THE FIRSTBORN of MAN and BEAST! Death would be upon the FIRST-BORN one way or another.

This was "the Gospel" to Israel, and Egypt. All who believed obeyed. All who accepted the message of the firstborn would make sure

that firstborn lamb was slain and that they
were covered and protected by the atoning
blood. They would be safe and secure under
the substitutionary death of this firstborn
lamb. They would put first things first! The
Gospel of "the lamb of God" was sounded
throughout Egypt. Whether they were Egyptians or Israelites, all must accept the message
of the firstborn lamb or come under Divine
judgment.

God sent nine plagues upon Pharaoh and
Egypt, but there was no response, only
continual hardening of the heart. Pharaoh
hardened his heart. God hardened Pharaoh's
heart. God will be to man, what man is to
Him.

The Lord told Pharaoh He would send one
last plague. It would concern the original
message Moses had received, which was the
message of "THE FIRSTBORN." God was
going to make Pharaoh willing to be willing.

What happened? At the midnight hour God
sent His angel through the land and every-
where DEATH struck the FIRSTBORN. The
firstborn had to die. The firstborn of Pharaoh,
the firstborn of the slave in prison, the firstborn
of all Egyptians, and the firstborn of all beasts
were struck by death. All must face this truth
of the firstborn, whether they like it or not.

Pharaoh and Egypt, as a national firstborn, rejected the lamb of God, a firstborn lamb, while Israel, God's national firstborn, accepted God's firstborn lamb. It was indeed firstborn for firstborn!

For Israel to be God's "Church of the First-born" they had to experience deliverance by the blood of the firstborn lamb. God had de-creed death on the firstborn. Either they would accept the death of a firstborn lamb and thus become God's "Church of the Firstborn," or else they would reject the death of this first-born lamb and be smitten as a firstborn nation. What a tremendous and fearful sight and night it must have been. As the Israelites went about preparing and slaying the firstborn lamb they inspected that lamb, knowing that it was a substitute for them. The firstborn lamb would die for the firstborn nation.

Perhaps we could digress for a moment here to examine another very important Scriptural principle. God, in the Old Testament, often had people do TYPICALLY what He Himself would do ACTUALLY. For instance, as we discussed earlier, Abraham had an only begot-ten son named Isaac (Hebrews 11:17-19). It was as if God said to Abraham, "Abraham, you are a father, and you have an only begotten son. I want you to offer your son typically, and illustrate what I, as a Father, will do actually with My Only Begotten Son" (John 3:16). Abraham did typically with his son in the Old Testament what God would actually do with His Son in the New Testament. The same is true here. In its offering of the Passover lamb, Israel shadowed forth typically many details which would be actually fulfilled in the offering up of the New Testament Paschal Lamb -- The Lamb of God (John 1:29,36).

John the Baptist said, *"Behold the Lamb of God, which taketh away the sin of the world"* (John 1:29). That was the message of the Firstborn Lamb of God. Israel kept its Paschal lamb for four days. This foreshadowed the truth that God would keep HIS LAMB, Jesus Christ, FOUR DAYS, i.e. four thousand years. Psalm 90:4 and II Peter 3:8 state that a day unto the Lord is as a thousand years and a thousand years as one day. From Adam to Jesus were four days of the Lord, i.e. four thousand years. Then in the evening of this day Jesus, God's Firstborn Lamb, the Firstborn of Mary, was slain for our deliverance. All must accept THE LAMB of God in order to become a member of the Church of the Firstborn. To reject the Lamb is to come under the judgment of the Death Angel, even as did the Egyptians, who rejected the Gospel of the

Passover lamb.

God spoke to Adam saying, "In THE DAY you sin you will surely die" (Genesis 2:17). Did Adam die in the 24-hour day or in God's 1000-year day? The answer is, both. He died spiritually at that moment in the 24-hour day when he sinned. He died physically 930 years later, within the 1000-year "day" of the Lord. No man has ever lived a complete "day" of the Lord as yet! All the old patriarchs died within the 1000-year day of the Lord. Methusaleh, though he lived to 969 years old, died within the "day" that the Lord had spoken of.

Israel kept their lamb for four 24-hour days, shadowing forth God's four 1000-year days which would pass before His Lamb would come to earth and die as the Paschal Lamb. In the Gospels we see how the political and religious leaders unwittingly fulfilled the details of the Passover Feast. Herod, Pilate, and Annas and Caiaphas, the High Priests, all inspected God's Lamb - Jesus - and found Him without spot, blemish or any such thing. Then they crucified God's Firstborn Lamb!

At the first Passover, the Israelites applied blood in a TRIUNE manner, on the two side posts and on the lintel. Surely all this pointed to the triune God -- Father, Son and Holy Spirit -- Who were involved in the deliverance

of a triune man -- spirit, soul and body! It was
one blood, but a threefold application of that
blood.

As well as the sprinkling of the blood, Israel
was to feed on the roasted body of that lamb,
unleavened bread and bitter herbs. They were
to eat it in haste and be ready to move out of
Egypt at the midnight hour. They were to be
"THE CHURCH" -- the ekklesia or CALLED
OUT ONES, the Church of the Firstborn.

If any Israelite dared to presume upon the
blood of sprinkling, to go outside the door of
the house and wander through Egypt, he
would have been met by the Death Angel (see
Exodus 12:22,23). Their safety and security
was "under the blood," and inside the DOOR
of the HOUSE. Typically, it points to that
security which is IN CHRIST (the Door) and
HIS CHURCH (the House)! The midnight
hour came and a great cry went up throughout
Egypt, as each uncovered house felt the
judgment of death on a FIRSTBORN one.
Again, this shadows forth the midnight cry of
the foolish virgins who do not have enough oil
to meet Christ, the heavenly Bridegroom (see
Matthew 25:1-13).

Israel had FAITH in the blood (see Hebrews
11:28). Egypt rejected that blood of the lamb
in UNBELIEF. Israel, like Abel, had faith in

the substitute lamb. Egypt, like Cain, manifested unbelief in that same lamb. Two firstborn nations were faced with the death of the
firstborn lamb -- one was saved, the other was
lost. Israel followed the faith of Abel, Seth,
Abraham, Isaac, and Jacob. Egypt followed
the unbelief of Cain, Ham, Ishmael, and Esau.
Israel realized that their salvation and choice to
be the Church of the Firstborn was based on
their faith in, and acceptance of, the firstborn
lamb. Jesus Christ is the FIRSTBORN of Mary
(Matthew 1:25). He is the beginning of the
creation of God (Revelation 3:14). He is the
FIRSTBORN of every creature (Colossians
1:15,18). He is the Head of the church, which
is His body. Naturally speaking, THE HEAD
IS FIRSTBORN (born first), and THE BODY
follows. Similarly, Christ is firstborn, born
first, and the church, His body, is following.

Jesus is the FIRSTBORN among a vast
family of sons (Romans 8:29), and believers are
the many sons. It is a many-membered body.

In Adam, that is, THE FIRST ADAM, we
lost everything. In Christ, THE FIRSTBORN
Lamb of God, we have all restored (see I Corinthians 15:21-23,45). Our first birth is the
natural birth of Adam and thus we are rejected
of God. But by accepting the Lamb of God we
come into spiritual birth, and thus become a

member of THE CHURCH OF THE FIRST-
BORN!

What a glorious pattern is set forth in Egypt
and Israel nationally, and then in the Passover
Lamb of redemption. The Church of the
Firstborn will be God's spiritual Israel because
of faith and acceptance of God's Divine Lamb,
the Lord Jesus Christ.

Chapter 4

Receipt Despite Deceit

L et us turn now to an examination of how the birthright flows on to and through Jacob, God's firstborn son.

"*And Jacob sod pottage: and Esau came from the field, and he was faint: And Esau said to Jacob, Feed me, I pray thee, with that same*

*red pottage; for I am faint.... And Jacob said,
Sell me this day thy birthright. And Esau said,
Behold, I am at the point to die: and what
profit shall this birthright do to me? And
Jacob said, Swear to me this day; and he sware
unto him: and he sold his birthright unto
Jacob. Then Jacob gave Esau bread and
pottage of lentiles; and he did eat and drink,
and rose up, and went his way: thus Esau despised his birthright"* (Genesis 25:29-34).

Here in Genesis 25 we see how Jacob bought
the birthright, the right of the firstborn, from
his brother Esau for the price of a bowl of soup.
Jacob did not deceive his brother, nor steal the
birthright from him; he simply bargained for
it. Esau despised his birthright and sold it for a
mess of pottage. The Scripture is very, very
clear on this matter. Jacob valued Divine
things; he valued spiritual realities.

We will also see in Genesis 27 how Jacob
deceitfully obtained the birthright blessing
from his father, Isaac. Then, Genesis 28 tells
us how Jacob received the promise of inheritance from the Lord Himself. Thus, the lesson
is evident. It was one thing for Jacob to buy
the birthright from Esau; it was another thing
to obtain, by deceit, the blessing from his
father, Isaac. Jacob may have been able to
buy the birthright, he may have been able to

gain the blessings from Isaac, but he could not force God to give him these things. God, however, overruled in the whole situation, because it was God's WILL for Jacob to receive the birthright, though Jacob's method was not God's WAY.

Returning to Genesis 27, we find that a number of years had passed since Jacob bought the birthright from Esau. We are told: *"And it came to pass, that when Isaac was old, and his eyes were dim, so that he could not see, he called Esau his eldest son, and said unto him, My son: and he said unto him, Behold, here am I. And he said, Behold now, I am old, I know not the day of my death: Now therefore take, I pray thee, thy weapons, thy quiver and thy bow, and go out to the field, and take me some venison; and make me savoury meat, such as I love, and bring it to me, that I may eat; that my soul may bless thee before I die"* (Genesis 27:1-4). Now it is evident that Isaac loved Esau because he did eat of Esau's venison, and also because Esau was the first-born after the flesh. The birthright was to go to the firstborn. Isaac, however, does not realize that this venison will be used in deceit. He does not know the day of his death, so he calls for Esau that he may pass on the birth-right inheritance to Esau through the laying on of hands and prophetic utterance.

In verse 5 and onward we see Rebekah plotting how to transfer this prophetic blessing over to Jacob. After all, she had received the word from the Lord BEFORE THE BIRTH of these sons that the elder would serve the younger (Genesis 25:23). She had the prophetic word, so she sought to "help God out."

It is remarkable to notice the weaknesses of human nature. Abraham received the promise of God that Isaac would be born in due time. Sarah, through IMPATIENCE, sought to help God fulfil His promises. (Hebrews 6:12 says that we *"through FAITH AND PATIENCE inherit the   promises"* -- not through faith and IMPATIENCE!) The end result was the birth of Ishmael, the FIRSTBORN AFTER THE FLESH, whom God had to set aside. Sarah, a woman of God, sought to help God out. Now here again, Rebekah, another woman of God, seeks to help God out, but by deception. She calls Jacob, God's firstborn, and tells him that his father is about to bless Esau with the birthright inheritance. She has the promises of God which were given before the birth of the twin sons. Jacob had bought the birthright. It looks as if the golden time has arrived; the whole thing could be lost if we do not help God out in the matter. No doubt she reasoned,

"God does His part, we have to do our part. God helps those who help themselves!"

Rebekah tells Jacob of the plan. He is to bring venison to his father, Isaac, and explain that the Lord(???) helped him get it so quickly. What can Jacob do? Does he not have to submit to his mother, as a submissive, obedient son? However, there is a problem and Jacob brings it up. He tells his mother that Esau is a hairy man, and he is a smooth man. If his father feels him, then he will discover the deception, even though he is almost blind. Instead of getting a blessing, Jacob will get a curse. Rebekah tells Jacob not to worry about this, saying, "Upon me be thy curse!" She was willing, foolishly, to invoke a curse upon herself for this deception. The tragedy is that, after Jacob had to flee from home, Rebekah never ever saw her favourite son again!

Rebekah takes Esau's hairy garment and places it upon Jacob. She makes the venison soup and gives it to Jacob. Jacob goes in before his father. Undoubtedly he is fearful. He knows he is acting out deception. He knows he is lying when he tells his father, "I am Esau, thy firstborn."

As for Isaac, he is going by his five senses. He is almost blind. He hears the voice, and it does not sound like Esau's. Then he FEELS

Jacob all over, and by the sense of feeling he is
deceived. Moving in the "sense realm" Isaac is
deceived. He is not judging by the spirit. He is
judging by feelings! How often we judge by
our senses and miss the mind of God. Jacob is
undoubtedly sweating it out. He is hoping his
brother Esau does not come in at any moment.
He is hoping his father Isaac doesn't want
another couple of bowls. When Isaac asks
Jacob how he obtained the venison so quickly
he says, "THE LORD brought it to me!" What
lying! What deception over a desire for spiritual things! When Isaac asks "Are you my very
son, Esau?," Jacob answers, "I am." Surely his
conscience was at work, accusing and con-
victing him.

Jacob would pay for this deception in the
years to come. The deceiver would himself be
deceived. Whatsoever a man sows, that shall
he reap. The laws of harvest are steadfast and
sure; they are irrevocable unless God Himself
revokes them.

Genesis 27:28,29 is the prophetic word, with
the laying on of hands, given by Isaac over
Jacob: *"Therefore God give thee of the dew of
heaven, and the fatness of the earth, and
plenty of corn and wine: Let people serve thee,
and nations bow down to thee: be lord over
thy brethren, and let thy mother's sons bow*

*down to thee: cursed be every one that curseth
thee, and blessed be he that blesseth thee."*
The Holy Spirit, through the writer to the
Hebrews (Hebrews 11:20), tells us, *"By FAITH
Isaac blessed JACOB and ESAU concerning
things to come."* This shows that God overruled in the total situation. His sovereignty
overruled in the affairs of men. He permitted
these events to happen. However, God would
deal drastically with Jacob in the years to come
before he could inherit the fulness of THE
BIRTHRIGHT INHERITANCE which belongs
to THE FIRSTBORN.

This passage gives us an example of the laying on of hands and prophecy, part of the first
principles of the doctrine of Christ (see
Hebrews 6:1-2). Isaac laid hands on Jacob,
and prophesied over his own son concerning
things to come. This was done in faith, in spite
of deception on the part of Rebekah and Jacob.

Returning to Genesis 27, from verse 30
onward, we see that Isaac has just finished blessing Jacob when Esau returns from the field
with the venison. After making the soup he
goes in to his father to receive the blessing of
the firstborn. Isaac trembles as he realizes the
deception which has taken place. He realizes
he has spoken the WORD OF THE LORD and
it cannot be reversed, nor can it be recalled.

Esau lifts up his voice and weeps. He cries
with a loud and exceedingly bitter cry. The
past years sweep over him: He had despised his
birthright years before, he sold it to Jacob, so
Jacob really is entitled to it. No doubt Esau
never did tell his father about it, but God saw
it, and now his father has blessed Jacob with
the birthright inheritance!

In verse 36 Esau laments over two things:
"And he said, Is not he rightly named Jacob?
for he hath supplanted me these two times: he
took away my BIRTHRIGHT; and, behold,
now he hath taken away my BLESSING. And
he said, Hast thou not reserved a blessing for
me?" Thus we have *THE BIRTHRIGHT* and
THE BLESSING, the two things that belonged
to the firstborn. Jacob bought the birthright
from Esau, his brother, and then he obtained
the blessing from his father Isaac. It was the
prerogative of the father to pass on the inheritance of the birthright and Isaac had blessed
Jacob. The word had gone forth out of his
mouth and it could not be reversed. Isaac gave
Esau A blessing, but not THE blessing! It is this
tragic scene which the writer to the Hebrews
takes up in Hebrews 12:16,17: *"Lest there be*
any fornicator, or profane person (one who
speaks lightly of sacred things), *as Esau, who*
for one morsel of meat sold his birthright. For

*ye know how that afterward, when he would
have inherited the blessing, he was rejected:
for he found no place of repentance, though he
sought it carefully with tears."*

Esau wept too late. He sought the place of
repentance, and a way to change his father's
mind, but too late. He despised the sacred
birthright earlier and it was too late now. The
writer to the Hebrews is speaking to Spirit-
filled believers. He is warning them not to be
like Esau and not to sell their spiritual birthright. It is sad to say there are many "Esau
believers" who are selling out their birthright
by the lusts of the flesh, and by profanity.
They are selling out for "a mess of pottage" --
for temporal satisfaction. These people do not
properly value eternal realities. There will
come that terrible "afterward" in due time,
and what tears of regret will flow, but it will be
too late to receive their birthright then. God
gives every person a space to repent, but once
that space is over it is too late to repent (Revelation 2:21). The "space" means a period of
time. No one but God knows how long that
period of time is. We enter life by birth and
we leave by death; the period of time in
between is the "space" God gives to man.
What we do in that space is important, for time
and eternity. Birth is the door into life, and

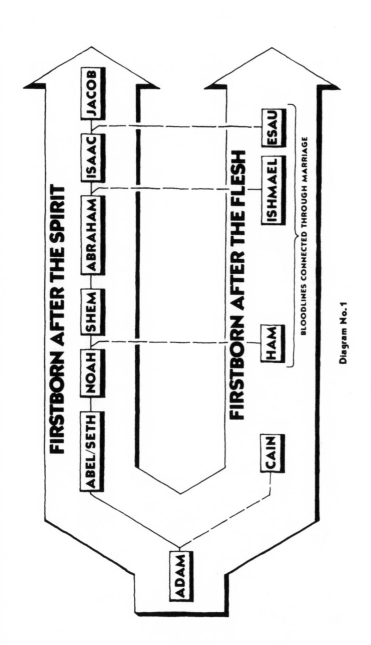

FIRSTBORN AFTER THE SPIRIT

ABEL/SETH · NOAH · SHEM · ABRAHAM · ISAAC · JACOB

ADAM

FIRSTBORN AFTER THE FLESH

CAIN · HAM · ISHMAEL · ESAU

BLOODLINES CONNECTED THROUGH MARRIAGE

Diagram No. 1

death is the exit door. Temporal and fleshly satisfaction is not worth the tragic consequences of selling out the birthright inheritance of God.

In Genesis 28 Jacob is forced to flee from home because of his brother's hatred for him over the loss of the birthright blessings. At Bethel God meets with Jacob and in His grace confirms to Jacob that He was the Giver of the birthright inheritance, and would work things out in His own sovereign plan.

Therefore, in God's mind Jacob is THE FIRSTBORN, the holder and dispenser under God of THE BIRTHRIGHT INHERITANCE!

Diagram No. 1 on the page facing brings together what we have covered so far. A glance over this diagram shows the pattern of the firstborn and to whom the birthright inheritance was given. Up to this point the pattern of God has been quite simple -- the birthright has simply gone to that individual of the pair who is firstborn in God's eyes. In the next chapter, however, we will examine a situation in which the passage of the birthright becomes considerably more complicated.

Chapter 5

Distributing
to the Deserving

We come now to Jacob and his twelve
sons. The book of Genesis closes with
the account of Jacob's prophetic words
to these sons. A serious consideration of Genesis
chapters 48-49 shows that Jacob, under God, is
passing on the birthright inheritance to his sons,

especially that which pertains to the firstborn.
Which of them is THE FIRSTBORN in God's
mind? To whom should THE BIRTHRIGHT
go? Who should get THE BLESSING? These
are the questions Jacob has to grapple with in
discovering the mind of the Lord God. We
will find some distinctive truths regarding the
firstborn and the birthright as we consider the
account of this situation.

The Firstborn Pattern

It cannot help but be noticed that, even in
the marriage of Jacob and the birth of his
twelve sons, the firstborn pattern is revealed
again. Jacob desired Rachel to be his beloved
wife, so he asked Laban, her father, for her.
However, when the evening of the marriage
had passed and Jacob woke in the morning, he
discovered that Laban had deceived him in the
matter of his wife. Although Jacob wanted
Rachel, the one he really loved, Laban had
given him Leah, THE FIRSTBORN, and
withheld Rachel. Laban said it was their
custom that the firstborn must be given in

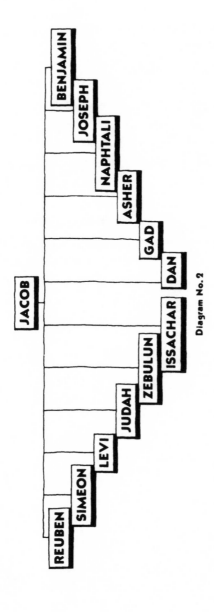

Diagram No. 2

marriage before the younger. Thus Jacob received the firstborn in marriage.

As we study the book of Genesis further with relation to the birth of Jacob's twelve sons, we see another remarkable confirmation of this firstborn pattern.

From LEAH, the firstborn daughter of Laban, we have these sons: Reuben, Simeon, Levi and Judah; next we have Gad and Asher, born of Leah's handmaid. Then, of Leah again, we have Issachar and Zebulun. From Rachel's handmaid we have Dan and Naphtali, but *from RACHEL* we have Joseph and finally Benjamin. From Leah and her handmaid we have eight sons in all, but from Rachel and her handmaid we have four sons (see Genesis 35:23-26).

The remarkable thing about these sons is that *REUBEN was the firstborn of Leah*, who was the firstborn daughter, while *JOSEPH was the firstborn son of Rachel*. Rachel was Jacob's "first love." Joseph is Jacob's ELEVENTH son. The eleventh son is also a firstborn son!

This pattern of God is so simple yet so marvelous in its implications.

We come now to the passing on of the birthright to God's firstborn under the hands of Jacob and the God of Jacob. We see how Jacob, as a man of faith under the direction and guidance of the Holy Spirit, prophesies over his sons and passes on the blessings of the birthright to the firstborn of God's choice.

In Genesis 49:1 and 2 we read: *"And Jacob called unto his sons, and said, Gather yourselves together, that I may tell you that which shall befall you in the last days. Gather yourselves together, and hear, ye sons of Jacob; and hearken unto Israel your father."* Now, by the laying on of hands and prophecy, he begins to prophesy over his own sons the mind of God. Picture the scene as Jacob has his twelve sons about him and, moving in the Spirit of God, begins to give the prophetic word, a word which will affect the destiny of the nations and tribes which will come from these sons.

Reuben —
The Firstborn
After the Flesh

"Reuben, thou art my firstborn, my might, and the beginning of my strength, the excellency of dignity, and the excellency of power: Unstable as water, thou shalt not excel; because thou wentest up to thy father's bed; then defiledst thou it: he went up to my couch" (Genesis 49:3,4). What a terrible prophecy over Reuben! It will be noted that Reuben is the FIRSTBORN AFTER THE FLESH, but he is to be set aside because of his sins.

The characteristics of Reuben are immorality, instability and defilement. Jacob had not forgotten, and neither had the Lord God, the terrible sin Reuben committed by defiling Jacob's concubine (see Genesis 35:21-22). It seems Jacob said nothing back then, but now the time has come for the passing on of the birthright. Reuben forfeits it because of his terrible sin of fornication.

It should be remembered that Esau was a

fornicator who sold his birthright. Reuben also is a fornicator and loses the birthright. Thus Reuben manifests the carnal characteristics of Esau, the firstborn. The writer to the Hebrews warns Spirit-filled believers of falling into the same sin and losing the birthright also (see Hebrews 12:15,16).

In I Chronicles 5:1,2 we have further confirmation of the rejection of Reuben as the natural firstborn because of his sin. *"Now the sons of Reuben the firstborn of Israel, [for he WAS the firstborn; but, forasmuch as he defiled his father's bed, HIS BIRTHRIGHT WAS GIVEN UNTO THE SONS OF JOSEPH THE SON OF ISRAEL: and the genealogy is not to be reckoned after the birthright. For Judah prevailed above his brethren, and of him came the chief ruler; but the birthright was Joseph's...."* What lessons there are for all believers here in these verses. There are Christians today who, like Esau and like Reuben, are selling their spiritual birthright over the lusts of the flesh -- over fornication and other forms of immorality. God is a holy God and He hates sin. He is not only a God of love, but also a God of holiness.

The Scripture shows that when a person is born again he is born into the spiritual Israel of God and placed in one of the spiritual tribes of this spiritual Israel. We are brought into the commonwealth of Israel, the twelve-tribed spiritual Israel (see Galatians 6:16). They are not all spiritual Israel which are of national Israel (see Romans 9:6-9).

Paul strongly warns the believer against defiling the temple of God by fornication, and says that God will DESTROY his body, which is the temple of the Holy Spirit, should he defile it (see I Corinthians 6:12-20). So great a danger is there for believers who defile themselves-- the danger of forfeiting their spiritual birthright in God! Though God forgives, yet He allows the law of harvest -- of sowing and reaping -- to continue. David sinned grievously. The Lord forgave, and David was pardoned -- but also PUNISHED! It was not worth the few moments of physical gratification to have the twenty years of Divine chastening in his house. We cannot abuse the grace of God and expect to get away with it.

Returning to our narrative, we find that Jacob, like his father Isaac, is failing in eyesight, but he can see spiritually. Though natural blindness seems to be upon him, spiritual blindness is not there. Reuben, the firstborn after the flesh, is sovereignly set aside, so the birthright must pass on to another son. The Divine pattern continues.

Judah —
The Sceptre

Naturally speaking, the birthright should have been passed down to the next son or sons. Thus, it should have gone to Simeon, or Levi. However, notice the prophetic word over these sons in Genesis 49:5-7: *"Simeon and Levi are brethren; instruments of cruelty are in their habitations. O my soul, come not thou into their secret; unto their assembly, mine honour, be not thou united: for in their anger they slew a man, and in their selfwill they digged down a wall. Cursed be their anger, for it was fierce; and their wrath, for it was cruel: I will divide them in Jacob, and scatter them in Israel."* Note the characteristics of these sons: Anger, selfwill and wrath! Reuben lost the birthright because of fornication and instability, while Simeon and Levi are noted for anger, wrath and selfwill. They brought reproach on their father Jacob in the slaying of a man, so the birthright by-passes them. Simeon is placed first as the ringleader. Later on we will see that Levi actually does receive a part of the birthright for a Divine reason.

The next son in line for the birthright is

JUDAH! *"Judah, thou art he whom thy brethren shall praise: thy hand shall be in the neck of thine enemies; thy father's children shall bow down before thee. Judah is a lion's whelp: from the prey, my son, thou art gone up: he stooped down, he couched as a lion, and as an old lion; who shall rouse him up? The sceptre shall not depart from Judah, nor a lawgiver from between his feet, until Shiloh come; and unto him shall the gathering of the people be"* (Genesis 49:8-10). The full passage, verses 8-12 should be read concerning Judah. Consideration of these verses shows that *part of the birthright* promises are given here to Judah. We should remember I Chronicles 5:1,2 where we saw that Reuben was the firstborn of Israel, but his birthright was given to *Joseph* and his sons. *Judah* is given the promise of rulership and kingship, that is, the Messianic seed line was to come out of the tribe of Judah. From the tribe of Judah would come the kings of Judah, and eventually THE KING OF KINGS AND LORD OF LORDS, Jesus Christ Himself (see Revelation 5:5). Judah would have the natural, national line of kings, and also the spiritual King, even Jesus Christ Himself, the Lion of the tribe of Judah, and the Root of David (see Romans 1:3). Jacob finishes blessing Judah and moves along.

Joseph —
The Birthright

Let us by-pass all the other sons of Jacob and go down to Joseph. Suffice it to say that each of the other sons do receive a prophetic blessing, whether they be proper sons of the proper wives or sons born of the handmaids. However, it is *JOSEPH* whom the Lord Himself, through Jacob, chooses to be the *firstborn after the Spirit*.

In Genesis 49:22-26 we have Jacob's blessing over Joseph himself. Although this passage is too full to study here, it should be read carefully, for in it we see the tremendous prophetic blessing given to Joseph, and also the Divine reason for this blessing. Joseph is a fruitful bough by a well. His branches will run over the wall. Though he had been sorely shot at and grieved, yet his strength was in God, the Shepherd and Stone of Israel. Joseph would be blessed with all the blessings of heaven above and earth beneath. The remarkable expression is given that Joseph *"was separate from his brethren"* (Genesis 49:26).

Joseph's life is characterized by that which is of God. There is no fault recorded against this

son of Jacob. He also is a remarkable type of
Christ as the beloved and rejected and exalted
son, seeking reconciliation with his brethren
who sold him out.

Again, we must note I Chronicles 5:1,2,
where we are told that the birthright was taken
from Reuben and given to the sons of Joseph.
The details of this are dealt with in Genesis 48
where Jacob blesses the sons of Joseph. Notice
again the Divine principle of the firstborn after
the flesh and the firstborn after the Spirit, even
in the blessing of these two sons of Joseph.

In Genesis 48:5 Jacob says to Joseph, *"And
now thy two sons, EPHRAIM and MANAS-
SEH, which were born unto thee in the land of
Egypt before I came unto thee into Egypt, are
mine; as REUBEN and SIMEON, they shall be
mine."* Notice the pattern. Reuben lost the
birthright. Simeon also forfeited it. Now
Joseph's two sons are brought in, sons of
Rachel, sons of Jacob. Jacob says that
EPHRAIM and MANASSEH will be to him as
REUBEN and SIMEON once were. That is,
they will become part of the nation of Israel,
adopted into the tribes, and thus receive tribal
inheritance. They will be called after the
name of their brethren in their inheritance,
that is, they will be *ISRAELITES!*

Let us go to verses 10-16 of Genesis 48 where

Joseph brings these sons to Jacob to receive the
blessing. Joseph brings Manasseh, who is the
firstborn after the flesh of Joseph, to Jacob's
right hand for blessing. He brings Ephraim,
the younger brother, to Jacob's left hand for
blessing by the laying on of hands.

Suddenly, as Jacob is about to bless prophet-
ically, *he crosses his hands*, placing his right
hand on Ephraim's head. Joseph is displeased,
thinking of his father's age and physical blindness. He endeavours to tell Jacob that
Manasseh is the FIRSTBORN. Jacob replies
that he knows it, but God has chosen it to be
the other way. *EPHRAIM* is to be the *FIRST-
BORN* in God's mind and receive the inheritance of the firstborn.

Undoubtedly Jacob remembered when he
deceived his own father regarding the birthright blessing when his father's eyes were also
dim. Now, however, Jacob is in the Spirit,
moving in faith as he blesses both of the sons of
Joseph (see Hebrews 11:21). Jacob invokes the
triune name of Abraham, Isaac and Jacob/
Israel over these two sons as they are adopted
into the Israel of God. All of this finds its New
Testament fulfilment in baptism in the name of
the eternal Godhead -- the name of the Father,
and of the Son, and of the Holy Spirit -- and
also in the triune name of the Lord Jesus Christ

(see Matthew 28:18-20 with Acts 2:34-36). It is all through the cross of our Lord Jesus Christ that blessing comes. The blessings over these sons should be read in Genesis 48. Ephraim now becomes the firstborn and is to become a great nation and a company of nations. Manasseh also is to become a great nation. However, Ephraim is set before Manasseh and given a greater portion of blessing (see Genesis 48:15-22). This part of the birthright included multiplicity of seed as well as the material blessings of earth and heaven.

Let us summarize the truths we have discovered in this chapter:

* Jacob is the holder and dispenser of the birthright, under God. He may pass it on to any of his sons, as the Lord God directs.

* Reuben, the firstborn after the flesh, is set aside. He forfeits the birthright because of fornication and instability.

* Simeon also forfeits the birthright because of evil character qualities.

* Levi, as will be seen, is given a part of the birthright inheritance.

* Judah is given a part of the birthright inheritance, especially with relation to rulership and Messianic seed-line promises.

* Joseph is given part of the birthright inheritance, especially through his two sons, Ephraim

and Manasseh. Jeremiah the prophet cries out from the Lord God: *"Ephraim is my firstborn"* (Jeremiah 31:9).

In our final chapter we will discover more truths from the account of Jacob and his sons, and see how these truths apply to today's believer. However, to this point we have seen that the pattern continues. The firstborn after the flesh is not necessarily the firstborn after the Spirit. God is the One Who chooses His firstborn. God is the One Who gives the birthright!

There will be a CHURCH OF THE FIRST-BORN which will receive THE BIRTHRIGHT inheritance; it will be the church of God's choice, the church of Divine Character.

Chapter 6

The Spiritual Birthright

THE NATURAL BIRTH AND THE SPIRITUAL BIRTH

John 3:1-21 is the account of when Jesus spoke to Nicodemus, a ruler of the Jews. Nicodemus came to Jesus by night and acknowledged that he believed Jesus was a teacher come from God, this being attested to by the miracles which He did.

Jesus by-passed these remarks and told
Nicodemus that what was needed was "new
birth." He said, *"Ye must be born again* (from
above)." Nicodemus listened with the natural
ear and interpreted this statement accordingly.
He asked Jesus how anyone could be "born
again." Could a person enter into his mother's
womb a second time and be "born again?"
Jesus answered (verse 12) that if Nicodemus did
not understand *"earthly things"* how could he
ever understand *"spiritual things?"* Earthly
things point to heavenly and spiritual things.
The natural birth, the birth after the flesh,
points to the spiritual birth, the birth after the
spirit. *"That which is born of the flesh is flesh;
and that which is born of the Spirit is spirit"*
(v.6).

The pattern of the firstborn has exemplified
this truth over and over again. Our studies of
Old Testament characters have shown that
there are two lines, the Godly and the ungodly.
The ungodly line, "the firstborn after the flesh"
speaks of the "natural birth," which is our birth
through the line of Adam, the first man. The
lives of these firstborn ones manifest the evil
characteristics of the failen, Adamic nature,
since they have only been born of the flesh.
The nationality or background of the flesh does
not matter -- *flesh can only produce flesh.*

That which is born of flesh, whether Jewish flesh or Gentile flesh, is flesh. One can belong to a denomination (or a non-denominational denomination), yet never belong to CHRIST'S CHURCH. All fallen flesh, even "religious" flesh, is set aside by God that He might bring in the spiritual firstborn.

We have also seen, in the pattern of the first-born, those who were accepted by God as born of the Spirit. The Godly characteristics of those who were "firstborn after the Spirit" are the same as those of the "born again" ones. *"He that is joined unto the Lord is one spirit"* (I Corinthians 6:17). *"That which is born of the Spirit is spirit"* (John 3:6b). *"The Spirit itself beareth witness with our spirit, that we are the children of God"* (Romans 8:16). Hence, those who have experienced the heavenly birth are accepted in God's mind as THE CHURCH OF THE FIRSTBORN, whose names are written in heaven!

Thus, we have discovered the answers to the questions we asked at the beginning of this book: "What is the Church of the Firstborn?" and "Who belongs to it?" The Church of the Firstborn is that true church which is made up of those who have been born of the Spirit of God. No one can be in this Church of the Firstborn unless he has experienced the heavenly, miracle birth. It is one thing to be born of man and quite another thing to be born of God. We have to know that we are *"born, not of blood, nor of the will of the flesh, nor of the will of man, but of God"* (John 1:13).

Being born again is being born of THE SPIRIT and THE WORD. Jesus said in John 3:5 that we must be born of the Spirit, while I Peter 1:23 says that we are to be born again of incorruptible seed, by the Word of God. Incorruptible seed refers to the spiritual birth, while corruptible seed speaks of the natural birth. As in natural birth there is the seed, the blood, the water and the spirit, so in spiritual birth there is the seed of the Word of God, the blood of Jesus, the water of regeneration and the renewing of the Holy Spirit (see also Titus 3:5).

The Natural Birthright and the Spiritual Birthright

We come now to consider the things that are involved in the birthright. The birthright belongs to the firstborn by right of birth. The natural sons of the Old Testament had a "natural birthright" passed on to them by their fathers. This arrangement was recorded as an example, pointing to the "spiritual birthright" which God has, in Christ, for every genuine believer. All persons born again do have a birthright to inherit. Again, it is "First the natural birthright, then afterward that which is spiritual."

Cain, Ham, Ishmael, Esau and Reuben have all shown that the firstborn after the flesh forfeits the birthright. Seth, Noah, Shem, Abraham, Isaac, Jacob, Judah, Joseph and Ephraim have shown that there is a birthright given by God to those whom He sovereignly chooses to be His firstborn.

The next question is, "What are the things which belong to the BIRTHRIGHT?" We will approach this question first from the natural, then afterward move to that which is spiritual. A consideration of the Old Testament accounts of the firstborn shows that there are five major things involved in the birthright, all of which must find their fulfilment in Christ and His church. The five things in the spiritual birthright are:

1. *The Ministry of Priesthood*
2. *The Rule of Kingship*
3. *The Prophetic Spirit*

4. The Double Portion Ministry
5. The Bruiser of the Serpent's Head
Let us consider these things in more detail.

The Ministry of Priesthood

The first area involved in the birthright is the ministry of a priest. The Scriptures attest to this.

You will recall that Genesis 49 describes Jacob blessing his sons by faith. As Jacob moves in the mind of the Spirit, in the laying on of hands and prophecy, God communicates His mind through him. He foretells the destinies of these twelve sons, who will eventually become the twelve tribes of Israel. We notice that as he prophesies concerning Simeon and Levi he says, *"I will divide them in Jacob, and scatter them in Israel"* (Genesis 49:7b).

God, in His foreknowledge, knew that in due time Levi would take on a special ministry among the tribes of Israel. Exodus 32 tells how the tribe of Levi eventually stood with Moses against the idolatrous golden calf worship that Aaron set up while Moses was on the holy mount. For this reason, at least, God gave part of the birthright to the tribe of Levi.

When we turn to Numbers 3:40-46, we find how the Lord gives Moses further instructions regarding the tribe of Levi and the birthright. This passage is a remarkable confirmation that Levi is to be given part of the rights of the FIRSTBORN. *"And the Lord said unto Moses, Number all the FIRSTBORN of the males of the children of Israel ... And thou shalt take the LEVITES for me [I am the Lord] INSTEAD of all the firstborn among the children of Israel; and the cattle of the Levites INSTEAD of all the FIRSTLINGS among the cattle of the children of Israel. And Moses numbered, as the Lord commanded him ... And the Lord spake unto Moses, saying, TAKE THE LE-VITES INSTEAD OF ALL THE FIRSTBORN AMONG THE CHILDREN OF ISRAEL, and the cattle of the Levites instead of their cattle; AND THE LEVITES SHALL BE MINE: I am the Lord."* This is very clear. The Lord here takes the tribe of Levi instead of all the firstborn of Israel to be His. This makes Levi a *firstborn* tribe unto the Lord. Although Levi was the third son of Jacob, yet God takes a part of the birthright of the firstborn and gives it to him.

Jacob prophesied that Levi and Simeon would be divided in Israel and scattered. Then

the Lord made it clear to Moses that Levi was
to be a firstborn tribe, taken instead of the
firstborn of the other tribes. Then in Deuteronomy 33:8-11 Moses prophesies positive confirmation that PRIESTHOOD MINISTRY is
the part of the birthright to be given to Levi.
This passage, Deuteronomy 33, is the account
of Moses blessing the twelve tribes. Jacob's
twelve sons have now become the twelve
tribes. Thus Moses prophesies: *"And of Levi
he said ... THEY SHALL TEACH JACOB
THY JUDGMENTS, AND ISRAEI, THY
LAW: THEY SHALL PUT INCENSE BE-
FORE THEE, AND WHOLE BURNT SAC-
RIFICE UPON THINE ALTAR. Bless, Lord,
his substance, and accept the work of his
hands: smite through the loins of them that rise
against him, and of them that hate him, that
they rise not again."* The division in Israel between Simeon and Levi had been foretold.
Now Moses prophesies that Levi would be
scattered in Israel, for they would become the
priestly tribe. Their ministry would be to
perform the priestly functions: burning incense, offering sacrifices, and teaching the laws
and statues of the Lord to other tribes of Israel.

All of this, plus subsequent revelation, confirms that the Levites became God's firstborn
and received a part of the birthright. *That*

part is PRIESTHOOD MINISTRY!

The concept of priesthood follows down through the patriarchs to Levi's priesthood:

* Adam was a priest as head of his house. This is implied in that God clothed Adam and Eve with coats of skin. *The skin* was the only part of the burnt offering the priest received, according to the instructions of the Lord given in Leviticus 7:8. The priesthood of Adam and Eve was thus confirmed when they were clothed with the skins of the sacrifice. Adam taught Cain and Abel the way of worship and sacrifice (see Genesis 4), knowledge which came from God's grace in redemption. Thus, the priesthood was passed on to the firstborn, the head of each new household.

* Noah was a priest unto God. He offered sacrifices on the altar to God at the time of covenant (see Genesis 8). He was a patriarchal priest.

* Job was also priest in his house. He offered sacrifices for his family unto God (see Job 1:1-5). He also was a patriarchal priest as head of his house.

* Abraham, Isaac, and Jacob were also priests unto God. They built altars unto the Lord and called on the name of the Lord, and God appeared in covenantal revelation to them (see Genesis 12-50).

Adam, Abel, Noah, Abraham, Isaac and Jacob -- all these speak of patriarchal priesthood. Each of these men are "firstborn" in the mind of God. Each had their family altar before the Lord. The very fact that these patriarchs were covenant men who built altars, offered sacrifices, and called upon the name of the Lord shows that they exercised priestly ministry. For this reason Jacob could pass on this part of the birthright to Levi, under God's direction.

Israel, as a nation, was God's son, God's firstborn. We see that in Exodus 4:22,23. In Exodus 19:1-6 God states His original intention that Israel, *AS A NATION*, be unto Him a *KINGDOM OF PRIESTS:* that is, a priesthood after the order of Melchisedec, which Abraham knew about. However, God dropped down to a secondary level, took out of the firstborn nation a firstborn tribe, and gave to this tribe part of the firstborn privileges -- priestly ministrations. Instead of the whole nation being a kingdom of priests, God chose a certain tribe -- the tribe of Levi with Aaron as its head, to be His priest.

IN APPLICATION, all born again believers are called to be "priests unto God" (see Revelation 1:6; 5:9,10; I Peter 2:5-9). Every believer is called to be a ministering priest. *This is part of the believer's birthright* -- priestly ministry unto the Lord. Every man should also be priest of his home, praying and interceding for his family, that they come to know the redemptive power of God. He should "take the lamb for the house" and know household salvation -- *"Believe on the Lord Jesus Christ, and thou shalt be saved, and thy house"* (Acts 16:31). The husband should be the head and priest of his home.

The Church of the Firstborn is called to be a priest unto God. Priestly ministry involves spiritual sacrifices and offerings. It involves worship and praise unto the Lord God. It involves intercessory prayer. It is the ministry of reconciliation and it involves ministry unto the Lord Himself. How many fail in these areas today because they let someone else do their priestly ministrations for them?

The Rule of Kingship

The next part of the birthright involves the rule of kingship, or the ministry of the king. Kingship speaks of ruling and reigning, of authority and power over all the power of the

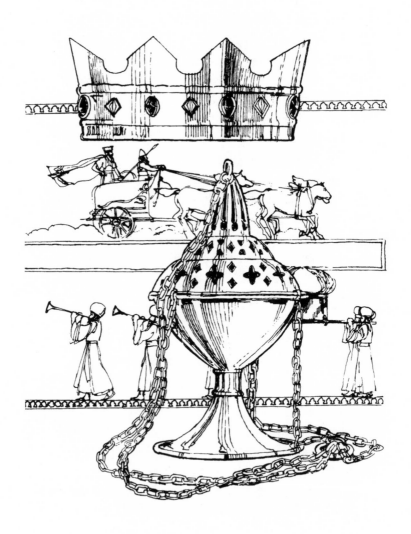

enemies of the kingdom.

This part of the birthright was given to Judah, the next son of Jacob. It is worthwhile to note that Jacob, instead of passing the full and complete birthright on to any one son, broke it up in parts, under God, to several sons.

Priesthood was given to Levi. *Kingship* is given to Judah. This is seen in the passage previously quoted, Genesis 49:8-12, where Jacob prophesied over his fourth son, Judah. We quote in part from this passage: *"The sceptre shall not depart from Judah, nor a lawgiver from between his feet, until Shiloh come; and unto him shall the gathering of the people be"* (v.10). Involved in this prophetic word is a twofold thought: There would be a natural line of kings holding the sceptre, and then there would come the King of kings, the Messiah, Who would be the Lion of the tribe of Judah.

There is little disputing of the fact that KINGSHIP RULE was given to Judah. The sceptre, which speaks of rulership, dominion, victory over enemies, headship, government, and lawgiving ministry, belonged to the tribe of Judah. This was his part of the birthright. However, one of the things most ministers and believers fail to see is that kingship had long been a part of the birthright, and that it was God's will for Israel to have a king in due time.

* Kingship was promised to Abraham at the time of covenant (Genesis 17:6).
* Kingship was promised to Sarah at the same time (Genesis 17:16).
* Kingship was promised to Jacob by the Lord (Genesis 35:11).
* Kingship was promised to the tribe of Judah through Jacob (Genesis 49:8-12).
* Kingship was also foretold by Moses (Deuteronomy 17:14-20).

Therefore, it was God's will for Israel to have a king, but it was not His time when Israel desired Saul. David was God's chosen king, from the tribe of Judah, in God's time and way.

This matter is also confirmed in I Chronicles 5:1-2, a passage which has already been dealt with. Let us look at it again in part: *"Now the sons of Reuben the firstborn of Israel, [for he was the firstborn; but forasmuch as he defiled his father's bed, his birthright was given unto the sons of Joseph .... FOR JUDAH PRE-VAILED ABOVE HIS BRETHREN, AND OF HIM CAME THE CHIEF RULER...."* Bible history abounds with accounts of the kings who came from the tribe of Judah and of the loins of David, the first king of Judah. This line consummates in Christ Jesus, the Son of David, Who is the King of kings and Lord of lords (see

Revelation 19:16).

Under the Old Testament, the priestly ministry and the kingly ministry were divided and separated to two different tribes, Levi and Judah. People who dared to presume to unite the offices of king and priest were judged by the Lord during the Old Testament times. King Saul, for instance, endeavoured to be a priest (see I Samuel 13:8-14) and lost the kingdom because of his presumptuousness. King Uzziah endeavoured to burn incense in the temple and to do that which pertained to the priesthood. He was smitten with leprosy for his sin of presumption (see II Chronicles 26:16-21).

In the New Testament, however, the two offices of priestly ministry and kingly ministry are brought together into one in the Person of Christ Jesus, and in His church. Jesus is a *KING-PRIEST* after the order of Melchisedec, and the church, that is, the CHURCH OF THE FIRSTBORN ones, is called to partake in that same order (see Hebrews 7). All believers are called to be *KINGS AND PRIESTS* unto God (see Revelation 1:6, 5:9,10; I Peter 2:5-9), indeed, a *ROYAL PRIESTHOOD*, or kingdom of priests. That which was offered to Israel, as a nation, by Moses in Exodus 19:1-6, is now presented to the spiritual Israel of God, the church, by Jesus Christ (see I Peter 2:5-9).

The church's ministry in this regard is to
exercise authority, government, law, and order
in the kingdom. This is part of the birthright
for the firstborn of God.

Let us note an interesting sideline to the
firstborn pattern and design as it relates to
Judah. In Genesis 38 we have the sad account
of Judah's sin relative to his own sons, who
were born from an evil relationship. Tamar,
who was the widow of Judah's son, Er, deceitfully played the harlot with her father-in-law,
Judah. As a result, in due time, she bore twin
sons by her own father-in-law. As the twin
sons were being born, one of them put out his
hand and the midwife tied a scarlet thread on
the hand of this *firstborn*. However, this son
withdrew his hand and the other son was born
first (firstborn!). This son, who was actually
born first, was named Pharez, while the other
child, whose hand was born first and received
the scarlet thread, was named Zarah. Again,
we find a changeover of the firstborn, even in
the sons of Judah by his daughter-in-law.

God saw this whole situation and, in His
wisdom, brought glory out of it. From the line
of Pharez came all the kings of Judah, including David, to the Messiah, while from the
Zarah line God carried on the natural line of
kings. Rahab, the harlot who helped the

Israelites with a scarlet thread, and who was saved by faith in their God (see Joshua 2:9-11 and Hebrews 11:31), married into the Pharez line (see Matthew 1:3-5) and became part of the genealogy of the Messiah. Oh, the wisdom and grace of God in all the failings of men.

We continue now with the final three parts of this glorious birthright.

The Prophetic Spirit

The next part of the birthright to be considered is The Prophetic Spirit. This portion also includes the ministry of the prophet. The prophetic spirit was evidently manifested in the elect of God in the former dispensation, for prophecy and prophets were a great part of the Old Testament times. The Prophetic Spirit is seen to be part of the birthright, the inheritance of God to His firstborn ones.

In Hebrews chapter eleven we have the "Heroes of Faith" listed: Abel, Enoch, Noah, Abraham, Isaac, and Jacob, as well as a number of others. It is significant to note that each of these were "firstborn" in the eyes of God. To them were given the portions of the

birthright which we are considering; among
them we see the prophetic spirit.

* Adam had the prophetic spirit upon him
when he prophesied concerning his bride. This
is confirmed by Paul in Ephesians 5:31,32,
where he uses the very words of Adam, and
then says, *"This is a great mystery: but I speak
concerning Christ and the church."*

* Noah had the prophetic spirit upon him also.
He foretold the coming judgment by the Flood,
and the preservation of a Godly remnant in the
ark of salvation.

* Enoch also had the prophetic spirit upon
him. He foretold the second coming of Christ
(see Jude 14, 15), leaping over dispensations
down to the last days.

* Abraham is the first person called a prophet
in Scripture (see Genesis 20:7).

* Isaac certainly had the prophetic spirit upon
him when he prophesied over Jacob and Esau
of things to come (see Hebrews 11:20).

* Jacob indeed had the prophetic spirit upon
him when he prophesied over his own sons as
well as Joseph's sons concerning future destinies
(see Genesis 48-49; Hebrews 11:21).

* Joseph, who also was firstborn in the eyes of
God and received the birthright, had the
prophetic spirit upon him. He foretold the
coming deliverance from Egypt and gave com-

mandment that his bones be taken into the promised land of Canaan (see Hebrews 11:22; Genesis 50:24).

Who can fail to see that in the line of God's firstborn ones, the prophetic spirit is seen? These were men who walked with God; they were covenant men; they were men of faith. They were "the firstborn," having the ministries of priest, king, and prophet united in one.

Jacob, under the anointing and insight of the Spirit of God, simply broke up the birthright into portions and passed them on to his sons.

When it comes to the prophetic spirit, and the ministry of the prophet, we find that all through the history of the nation of Israel, God raised up various prophets out of the various tribes that came from Jacob's sons. Jacob prophesied blessing upon his sons and the sons of Joseph, and from the tribes of these sons came the various prophets of God. Thus we may say that the prophetic spirit was poured out on different tribes of God's choosing throughout the course of Israel's history.

In the book of Judges, Samson came from the tribe of Dan, Deborah the prophetess from Ephraim, Gideon from Manasseh, and so on through to the New Testament, where we see that the prophetess Anna was from the tribe of Asher (see Luke 2:36). Judge-Deliverers,

Prophets, and those who prophesied also arose out of the other sons of Jacob in their tribal histories.

IN APPLICATION, we see that part of the spiritual birthright is the prophetic spirit. In the New Testament, God promised that His Spirit would be poured out on all flesh, as Joel had said (Acts 2:17-34; Joel 2:28-32). Paul said that ALL God's people may prophesy; the gift of prophecy is spoken of in I Corinthians 14, as well as the ministry of the prophets. Not all will be in the office of a prophet, which is spoken of in Ephesians 4:11, but all may have the prophetic spirit upon them, whether sons or daughters, handmaidens or servants. The doctrine of the laying on of hands and prophphecy (see Hebrews 6:1,2) also has its place in this portion of the birthright. There are those who despise prophesyings, but the Church of the Firstborn will have the prophetic spirit upon it more and more as the coming of the Lord Jesus Christ approaches. The testimony of Jesus is the spirit of prophecy (see Revelation 19:10).

We are living in the last of the last days when the spirit of prophecy is falling upon God's people. It is a portion of the spiritual birthright for each member of the Church of the Firstborn.

The Double Portion

The next part of the birthright is that which is referred to as "The Double Portion." This term can apply to a variety of the blessings of God upon His people.

Let us look at a very important Scripture which speaks of the double portion being given to the firstborn. In Deuteronomy we read the following laws concerning the firstborn: *"If a man have two wives, one beloved, and another hated, and they have born him children, both the beloved and the hated; and if the firstborn son be her's that was hated: Then it shall be, when he maketh his sons to INHERIT that which he hath, THAT HE MAY NOT MAKE THE SON OF THE BELOVED FIRSTBORN BEFORE THE SON OF THE HATED, WHICH IS INDEED THE FIRST-BORN: BUT HE SHALL ACKNOWLEDGE THE SON OF THE HATED FOR THE FIRSTBORN, BY GIVING HIM A DOUBLE PORTION OF ALL THAT HE HATH: for he is the beginning of his strength; THE RIGHT OF THE FIRSTBORN IS HIS"* (Deuteronomy 21:15-17). This is so clear. The right of the

firstborn is a *DOUBLE PORTION* of the inheritance. Jacob followed the laws of the firstborn with the sons of Rachel and Leah. However, God saw the sins of Reuben, the firstborn, who thus forfeited the right of the firstborn. Then the birthright inheritance was broken up into portions and given to various sons.

Let us look at examples of the DOUBLE PORTION as given to THE FIRSTBORN. These things become prophetic and typical of the DOUBLE PORTION ministry which will be given to the Church of the Firstborn, to inherit in Christ.

* Joseph received a double portion of the birthright through his sons, Ephraim and Manasseh. Genesis 48:12-22 tells us how this blessing occurred. First Jacob crossed his hands before putting them on the boys' heads, thus indicating that the younger boy, Ephraim, was to be firstborn in God's eyes. Then Jacob *"blessed Joseph, and said, God...bless the lads; and let my name be named on them"* (vv.15a, 16b). Jacob's blessing upon both boys follows and, despite Joseph's objections, Jacob says of Manasseh, *"Truly his younger brother shall be greater than he"* (v. 19b). In conclusion, Jacob says to Joseph *"I have given to thee one portion above thy brethren"* (v.22a). God gives Joseph *the double portion* of the firstborn, though he

was not actually Jacob's firstborn, and He brings in Ephraim as Joseph's firstborn, giving this younger son the greater blessing.

* Elisha asked for a *double portion* of the spirit that was upon Elijah. Elijah was to be taken up by the Lord by way of translation. Elisha, his servant, had followed him faithfully. When Elijah asked him what he desired before he departed, Elisha said, *"Let a DOUBLE POR-TION of thy spirit be upon me"* (II Kings 2:9b). The marginal reading is, "the portion of the firstborn." (Read II Kings 2.)

* The manna which fell daily in the camp of Israel was but a daily portion -- one portion for each day. However, when it came to the sixth day God sent a *double portion* of manna, enough to carry them through the seventh day, which was the Sabbath day. Thus Israel received a double portion of bread for their needs (see Exodus 16).

What a tremendous part of the birthright is this! All the pictures of the double portion may be brought together for the Church of the Firstborn. There is a double inheritance, a double portion of the Spirit of God, and a double portion of the Bread of heaven for the church in these last days.

Notice that in II Kings 2:7,15-18 the sons of the prophets stood afar off to view Elijah and

Elisha, while Elisha hungered for the portion of the firstborn, the double portion, and stayed close to Elijah. The sons of the prophets were in their groups of fifty. Fifty is the number of "Pentecost." Many "pentecostal" people seem to stand afar off today. Nevertheless, God will have His "Elisha's" who will keep their eyes on Christ and fervently go after Him to receive the double portion inheritance. They will consti- tute the members of this Church of the First- born, and Christ's mantle will fall upon them. It was a hard thing Elisha asked (II Kings 2:10), but he kept his eyes on Elijah. Then Elisha saw the chariot and the horsemen thereof, and the mantle of God, the mantle of the double portion, fell to him. Elijah did eight miracles. Elisha did sixteen miracles. Truly, Elisha's was a "double portion" ministry!

The Early Church had its portion of the Holy Spirit, but the Last Day Church will have the double portion of that Spirit. Remember the principle, "the FIRST shall be LAST and the LAST shall be FIRST!" The double portion is truly part of the spiritual birthright.

The prophecy of Joel also gives another illus- tration of the double portion. Joel prophesies of the outpouring of the rains. These rains will be both the "early and the latter rains" in the first month; the floors will overflow with "corn, wine and oil" (see Joel 2:19,23,24). This is a double portion! *It is a double portion of rain and a double portion of harvest.* Rains and harvest are connected together.

The portion of the firstborn is a double portion. It is our spiritual birthright. There will be a double portion of inheritance, a double portion of the Spirit, a double portion of manna, and a double portion of rains and harvest. We are living in the close of the sixth day of the Lord, (see page 56), when the double portion is available to the church, the Church of the Firstborn.

Sadly, there are those who despise their birthright. They despise priesthood, kingship, prophecy, and the double portion blessings, and are selling out for a mess of pottage. What tragedy!

We come now to the fifth and final part of the birthright.

The Bruiser
of the
Serpent's Head

The fifth and final and most glorious part of the birthright is that which pertains to the bruising of the serpent's head; in other words, *THE SERPENT-BRUISER'S MINISTRY.* It speaks of the Satan-bruiser.

In Genesis 3:15 we have the first prophecy concerning this part of the birthright. God spoke to the serpent concerning the woman (Eve), who is a type of the church, the bride of Christ, saying: *"I will put enmity between thee and the woman, and between thy seed* (serpent's seed) *and her seed* (woman's seed); *it shall bruise thy head, and thou shalt bruise his heel."* In other words, there would come from THE WOMAN a particular seed which would bruise the head of the serpent. The serpent would bruise the heel, but then that same heel would turn around and bruise and crush the serpent's head. The very head that bruised the heel would in turn be crushed by that heel.

In Genesis 49:16,17 we have the prophecy of Jacob concerning Dan. This prophecy involved the fact that Dan would be *"a serpent by the way...that biteth the horse heels, so that his*

rider shall fall backward." What is this saying? Dan would be the first tribe to introduce
idolatry into Israel (see Judges 18:30). They
would bring the attack of the serpent into the
household of faith, the chosen nation, which
would bring about wholesale backslidings,
apostasy, in Israel. Thus, Dan would be doing
the work of the serpent, biting the heels. The
seed of the serpent would bruise the heel; the
serpent would cause the falling away. But the
head of the serpent would in due time be
crushed. The Lord said He would blot out the
name of the persons who brought idolatry into
Israel (Deuteronomy 29:18-20). It is for this
reason, no doubt, that the name of Dan is
missing from the 144,000 Israelites in the book
of Revelation. All things pertaining to the serpent are to be eliminated.

Let us briefly consider the theme of "the
serpent-bruiser" in the Scripture. I say briefly
because this theme is the theme of the whole
Bible. The Seed Who would bruise Satan's
head was to come through *a firstborn.*
* Abel was looked upon by Eve as her prophetic seed. When he was killed, God
appointed Seth to take his place (see Genesis
4:25).
* The seed promise continued on, by God,
through Noah (see Genesis 8-9).

* The seed promises were confirmed to and through Abraham, Isaac, and Jacob (see Genesis 12-50).

* The seed line is narrowed down to Judah, from whom the Messiah would come (see Genesis 49:8-12).

* The seed line followed through to David (see II Samuel 7:12-16).

* The seed line followed through to Mary, of whom Christ was born (see Matthew 1).

Genesis 3:15 foretold that the serpent-bruiser would be "the seed of the woman." The Seed of the woman is the virgin-born Son of David, of the tribe of Judah, Jesus Christ. At Calvary, the serpent bruised the heel of Jesus, the Messiah. However, with His resurrection, the Seed of the woman made possible the bruising of the head of the serpent.

There is a part in this bruising which is given to the church, that is, the Church of the First-born. Scripture shows that it is CHRIST AND HIS CHURCH together who bring about the ultimate bruising of Satan, the author of sin. This is confirmed by Paul in his epistle to the Romans. In Romans 16:20a Paul writes *"And the God of peace shall bruise Satan under your feet shortly."* In Genesis, God is talking to the woman as well as to the serpent. The woman is a type of the church; the serpent is symbolic of

Satan himself; Adam is a type of Christ. But the promise is given to "the woman" -- THE SEED OF THE WOMAN SHALL BRUISE the serpent's head! Thus, ultimately it is THE CHURCH, the bride of Christ--the Church of the Firstborn--which inherits the birthright.

Christ and His church are one -- one in ministry and one in inheritance; Christ and His church are the only agents in the world used in the casting out of devils, the healing of the sick, the ministry of reconciliation, and the forgiveness of sins. Christ is THE FIRSTBORN. He inherited the FULL BIRTHRIGHT and the firstborn ones He is joined to are joint heirs of that birthright with Him! Christ and His church together will be the Satan-bruiser which will crush eternally the serpent's head. Hallelujah!

Let us finish our study by looking at a remarkable Scripture in the book of Ezekiel.

Calvary — From Natural to Spiritual

All Bible expositors agree that Calvary's cross brought about a great transference of the natural to the spiritual, the temporal to the eternal, the shadow to the substance, the promise to the fulfilment, and the prophecy to the reality. This applies equally to the theme of the firstborn and the birthright.

The prophet Ezekiel proclaimed a remarkable prophecy. This prophecy had its natural and national fulfilment in Old Testament times, yet it also has spiritual reality for our times, especially in what happened at the cross of Jesus. *"And thou, profane wicked prince of Israel, whose day is come, when iniquity shall have an end, Thus saith the Lord God; Remove the diadem, and take off the crown: this shall not be the same: exalt him that is low, and abase him that is high. I will overturn, overturn, overturn it: and it shall be no more, UNTIL HE COME WHOSE RIGHT IT IS; and I will give it him"* (Ezekiel 21:25-27).

This prophecy said that iniquity would come to an end. The diadem (that is, the priestly mitre) would be removed. The kingly crown would be taken off. Things would not continue as before. The one who was high would be abased and the one who was low would be exalted. There would be an overturning of the priestly mitre and the kingly crown, and who would they be given to? They would be given to HIM WHOSE RIGHT IT IS, that is, they are given to Christ, Whose

BIRTHRIGHT it is!

It is recognized that there was a national fulfilment of this prophecy. However, it is the Messianic fulfilment we consider here. In the Old Testament period the priestly mitre was carried by the Aaronic priesthood and the kingly crown was worn by the kings of Judah. When Jesus came, Whose birthright it is, there was an overturning from the natural to the spiritual, from the Old Covenant to the New Covenant, from the earthly to the heavenly, from the temporal to the eternal. There is no longer the Mosaic Covenant or the Old Testament economy. All of that which was temporal was fulfilled at the cross. It is now overturned into that which is spiritual, that is, into Christ and His church. In former times Israel was the Church of the Firstborn. It was Israel which had the birthright broken up amongst its tribes. But now in New Testament times it is Christ and His church who receive the birthright.

In the comparison on the facing page we will see how all that was shadowed in Old Testament times finds spiritual fulfilment indeed in Christ and His church.

Jesus Christ is the HEAD of the church (Colossians 1:18). He is the Firstborn of Mary (Matthew 1:25). He is the Firstborn among

Christ - The Head

1) Christ is the Firstborn, the Head ....
2) Christ inherited the birthright ....
3) Christ is the Priest ....
4) Christ is the King ....
5) Christ is the King-Priest after the order of ....
   Melchisedec
6) Christ is the Prophet, WORD made flesh ....
7) Christ has the double portion ministry in all ....
   ways
8) Christ is the Satan-bruiser ....
9) Christ brought about the overturn from the ....
   natural to the spiritual

The Church - The Body

1) The church is firstborn, the body
2) The church is to inherit the birthright
3) The church is called to priestly ministry
4) The church is called to ruling ministry
5) The church is after the order of Melchisedec
   also, as Christ's body
6) The church has the prophetic spirit upon her
   and the WORD ministry
7) The church is also to inherit the double
   portion ministry in all ways
8) The church will see Satan bruised under its
   feet shortly
9) The church experiences the overturn from
   the Old Covenant to the New Covenant in
   Christ

many brethren (Romans 8:29), the Firstborn of every creature (Colossians 1:15), the First-born of the dead (Colossians 1:18), and the beginning of the creation of God (Revelation 3:14). In Him the full manifestation of the birthright was evidenced. He is the Priest, the King, the Prophet, and the Double Portion, and He is the Satan-bruiser. The fulness of the Godhead bodily is in Him as the Head of the church, but now this same fulness is to be manifested in HIS BODY, which is THE CHURCH -- The Church of the Firstborn (Ephesians 1:22,23). This fulness is to be manifested in the members of His body, for the body is to inherit that which is in the Head, even Christ. The church is to be in priestly and kingly ministry; the prophetic ministry is to be in it, as is the double portion ministry. Then, ultimately, Christ and His church will bring the crushing blow to that old serpent, the devil -- Satan himself (see Revelation 12).

Conclusion

The challenge comes to us. Will we follow in the line and ways of Cain, Ham, Ishmael,

Esau, Reuben and others who forfeited their
birthright as the firstborn after the flesh? Or
will we follow after Seth, Noah, Isaac, Jacob,
Judah and Joseph in the line of faith, and
inherit the birthright? Will we be as the Old
Testament Israel or the New Testament Israel?
There will be a church, the Church of the
Firstborn that will inherit the birthright. May
God give us grace to respond to Him, that He
may use us to build it! Amen and Amen!

About the Author

Born in Melbourne, Australia in 1927 and saved at the age of 14, Kevin Conner served the Lord in the Salvation Army until the age of 21. At this time he entered into pastoral ministry for a number of years. After that, he was involved in teaching ministry in Australia, New Zealand and for many years at Bible Temple in Portland, Oregon. After serving as Senior Minister of Waverley Christian Fellowship for eight years (1987-1994), he continued to serve the church locally as well as ministering at various conferences and the continued writing of textbooks.

Kevin is recognised internationally as a teaching-apostle after his many years in both church and Bible College ministry. His textbooks have been used by ministers and students throughout the world. He has been in great demand as a teacher and has travelled extensively. Kevin passed away peacefully in Melbourne, Australia in February 2019 at the age of 92.

Visit Kevin's web site at <u>www.kevinconner.org</u> for more details about his life and ministry, as well as information about his 65 books, his video courses, and his audio teaching podcast.

Other Books by Kevin Conner

Interpreting the Scriptures (Self Study Guide)

Interpreting the Symbols and Types

Jude, A Commentary

Keep Yourself Pure

The Kingdom Cult of Self

Kings of the Kingdom

Law and Grace

The Lord Jesus Christ our Melchizedek Priest

Maintaining the Presence

Marriage, Divorce and Remarriage

Messages from Matthew

Methods and Principles of Bible Research

Ministries in the Cluster

The Ministry of Women

Mystery Parables of the Kingdom

The Name of God

New Covenant Realities

Only for Catholics

Passion Week Chart

Psalms - A Commentary

The Relevance of the Old Testament to a New Testament Church

Restoration Theology

Revelation, A Commentary

Romans, A Commentary

Sermon Outlines

The Seventy Weeks Prophecy

Studies in the Royal Priesthood

The Sword and Consequences

The Tabernacle of David

The Tabernacle of Moses

The Temple of Solomon

Table Talks

Tale of Three Trees

This is My Story (Kevin Conner's autobiography)

This We Believe

Three Days and Three Nights (with Chart)

Tithes and Offerings

Today's Prophets

To Drink or Not to Drink

To Smoke or Not to Smoke

Two Kings and a Prince

Understanding the New Birth and the Baptism of the Holy Spirit

Vision of an Antioch Church

Water Baptism Thesis

What About Israel? (NEW)

Visit www.kevinconner.org for more information.

Visit www.amazon.com/author/kevinjconner for a list of other books by Kevin Conner.

The Key of Knowledge Seminar

Kevin Conner's popular "Key of Knowledge" Seminar is now available as an online teaching course. Part 1 covers 'Methods and Principles of Bible Research' and includes over 6 hours of video teaching, the required textbooks, extra hand out notes, and a self guided online study program.

Visit the course home page at www.kevinconner.org and select 'Courses' from the Menu for all the details. The first lesson, 'Challenge to Study' is FREE.

The second part of Kevin Conner's popular "Key of Knowledge" Seminar is also available as an online teaching course. While Part 1 covers Methods and Principles of Bible Research, Part 2 covers Interpreting the Bible and includes over 7 hours of video teaching, two downloadable textbooks, extra hand out notes, and a self guided online study program. These two courses can be taken as stand-alone courses, in succession, or simultaneously.

Kevin Conner's Audio Teaching

We are excited to announce a new podcast of Kevin Conner's teaching messages. This podcast is available directly from www.podbean.com (including on their mobile App) or from Apple Music or from within Spotify (if you are a subscriber).

Every week or so a message will be published, selected from messages Kevin has given over the years at various churches, conferences, and training seminars.

Be sure to subscribe so you are notified of recent releases.

Enjoy!

Kevin's Autobiography

Kevin Conner is known by many people around the world as a theologian, Bible teacher, and best-selling author of over 60 biblical textbooks. Although thousands of people have been impacted by his ministry and his writings, only a few people know his personal story. Kevin took the time to detail his own life journey, including lessons gleaned along the way, in his auto-biography "This is My Story" back in 2007. It is now available in three formats:

- Australian paperback from WORD books (www.word.com.au).
- International paperback from Amazon.
- eBook format from Amazon.
- PDF download - visit www.kevinconner.org/shop

Kevin was an orphan who never met his dad or mum. He grew up in boy's homes before coming to faith in Jesus Christ in the Salvation Army in his teenage years. From there, his life took many turns as he continued to pursue his faith in God and his understanding of the Scriptures and church life. Follow his journey and gain wisdom for your own life and ministry as you read his intriguing life-story.

PDF Versions of Kevin Conner's Books

Most of Kevin Conner's books are now available to purchase in quality PDF format. This format is in addition to the Kindle eBooks and paperback versions currently available. These PDF format editions are designed for people who live where there are no paperback versions available or who have no access to a Kindle eBook reader.

They are not for copying or redistribution.

You can order and pay for these PDF books at www.kevinconner.org/shop. Upon payment, a download link will be provided on the Check Out page and also via your email receipt.

Please note that all prices are in US dollars.